GW01373409

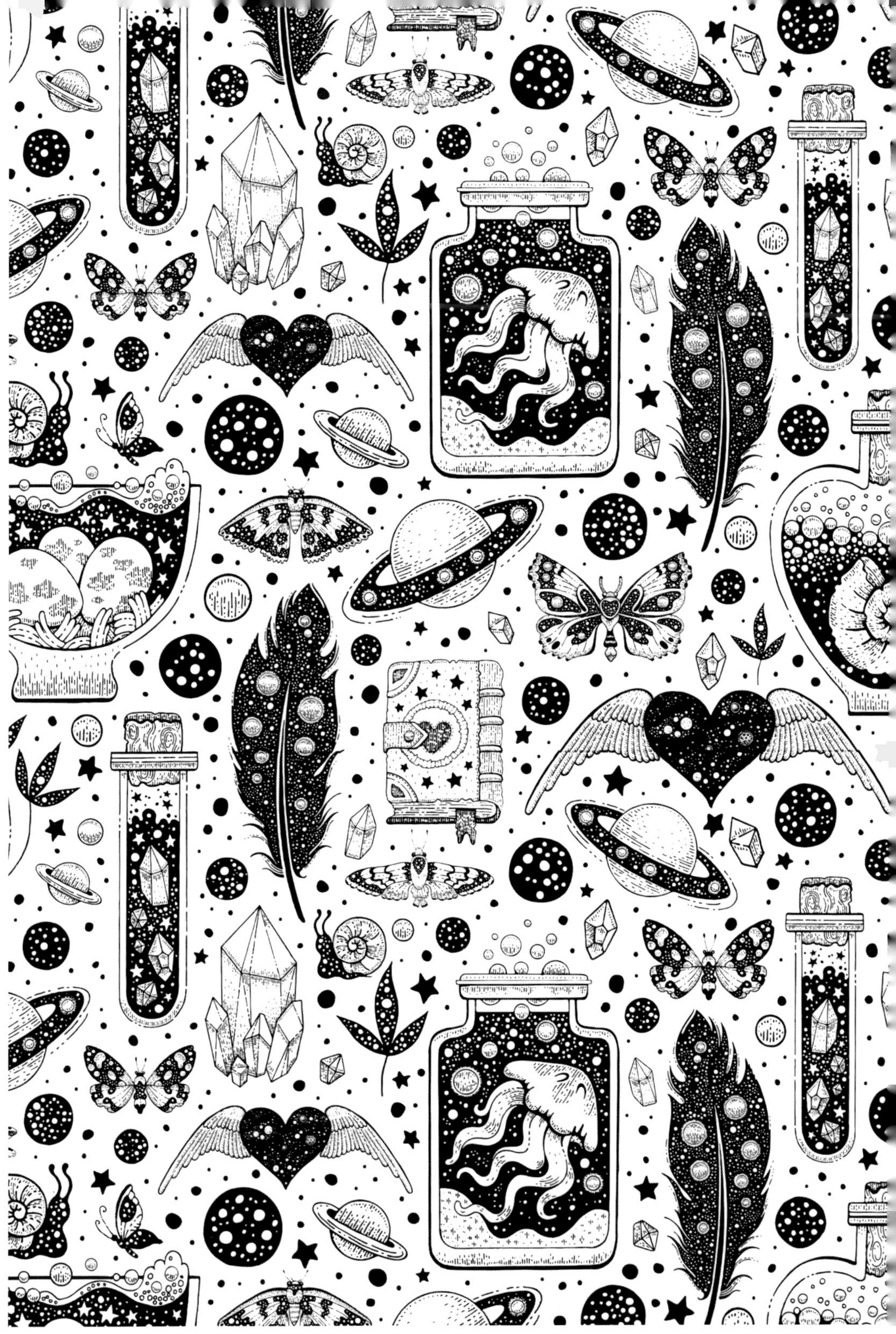

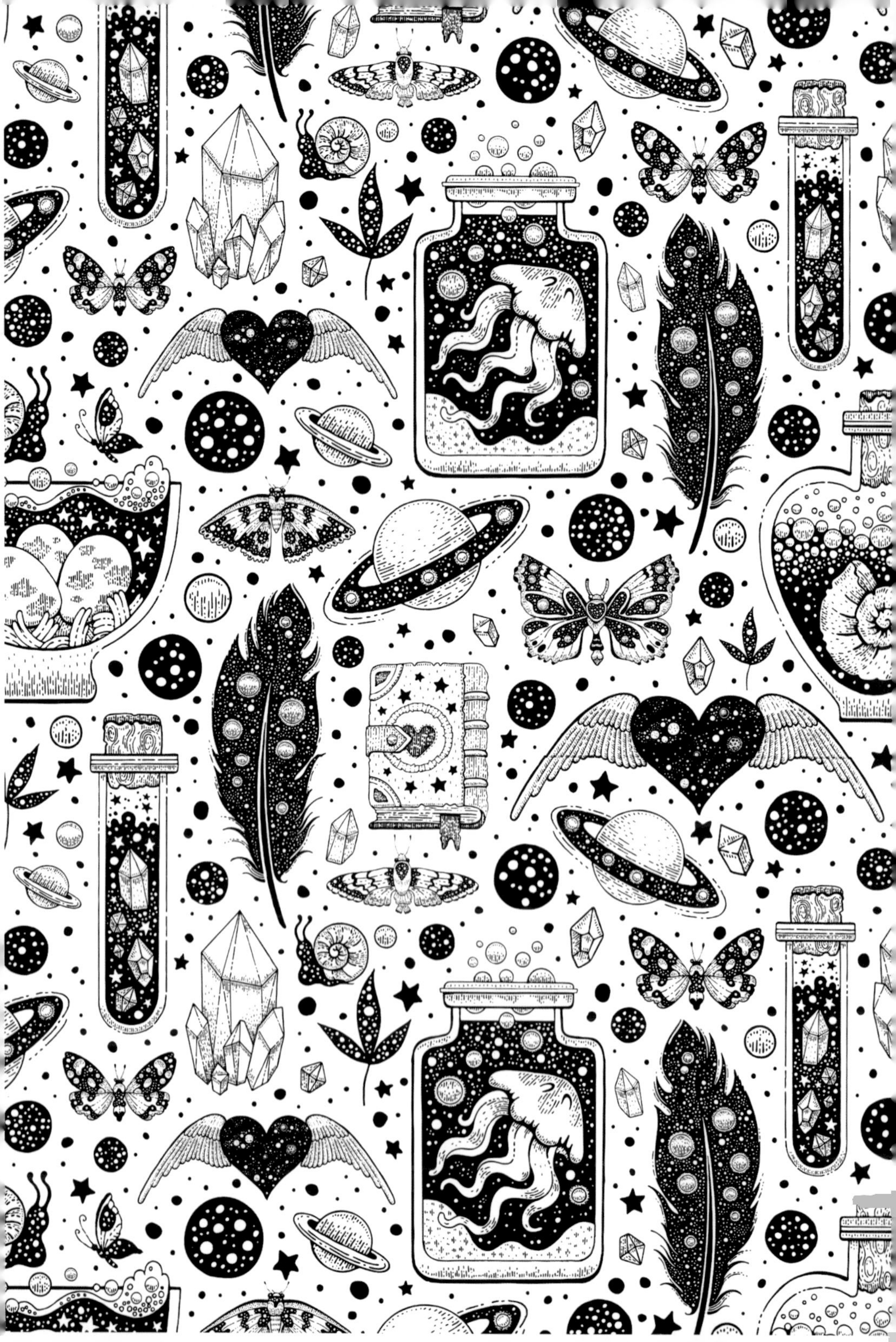

This Book Belongs To:

_____

_____

The Practicing Witch Diary

"The realm of witchcraft
is nothing short of transformative
—a journey that deeply, authentically,
and profoundly alters the course
of your life in the most beautiful of ways."

witchcraftspellsmagick.com

2025 Book of Shadows

The Practicing Witch Diary
Book of Shadows 2025

Northern Hemisphere Edition

Document your year of practicing witchcraft and beyond! Month by month, record all your magickal work, astrology, moon rituals, magickal correspondences, monthly altars, intention setting, manifesting, spell work, tarot notebook, dream journal, and so much more.

Witchcraft Spells Magick
witchcraftspellsmagick.com
WITCHCRAFT ACADEMY
Teaching Witches their Craft

The Practicing Witch Diary

witchcraftspellsmagick.com

2025 Book of Shadows

Greetings!

**The Practicing Witch Diary 2025 - Book of Shadows
is a space for documenting spells, rituals, divinations,
and encounters with the unseen realms.**

Recording your magickal journey offers a tangible account
of your spiritual growth, giving you the opportunity to reflect
on your progress and witness the transformation of your practice.

By focusing your energy and attention on the pages
of this journal, you will deepen your connection to the mystical,
manifest your written magick, and tap into your inner power.

Your written words, drawn forms, shapes, sigils,
and images are all conduits for manifesting change,
providing insights to reflect on your successes and challenges,
and continuously improving your skills as time passes.

Embrace the magick within and let it guide you on your journey.

**Blessed Be,
Bec Black**

The Practicing Witch Diary

© 2024 Copyright Witchcraft Spells Magick

The Practicing Witch Diary - Book of Shadows 2025
is a Witchcraft Spells Magick publication.
Published in 2024 for Witchcraft Academy,
owned and operated by Witchcraft Spells Magick.
www.witchcraftspellsmagick.com

Northern Hemisphere Hardback ISBN: 9780645830965
Southern Hemisphere Hardback ISBN: 9781763682801

Northern Hemisphere Paperback ISBN: 9780645830972
Southern Hemisphere Paperback ISBN: 9780645830996

Northern Hemisphere Digital ISBN: 9780645830989
Southern Hemisphere Digital ISBN: 9781763682818

YouTube: @WitchMusicPlaylist
Instagram: @witchcraftspellsmagick
Facebook: @witchcraftspellsmagick

Copyright text by Bec Black
Illustrations and original artworks by Bec Black
Additional illustrations sourced through image galleries

All rights reserved.

No part of this publication may be reproduced, stored, or transmitted in any form or by any means, including electronic, mechanical, photocopying, recording, or otherwise, without prior written permission from Witchcraft Spells Magick.

witchcraftspellsmagick.com

Coven

**Become part of an exclusive community
of witches in a private space on Patreon.**

Whether you're a seasoned practitioner or new to the magickal path,
this coven supports and enriches your practice in a welcoming environment.

Membership to the Witchcraft Academy Coven Includes:
A **Welcome Pack** with digital resources and an **Etsy store discount**
Monthly Witch Kit filled with new digital resources
Engage in discussions and share insights with like-minded souls
Access **loads** of exclusive **Practicing Witchcraft digital resources**
Lunar Cycle Reminders with **Moon Magick** guidance for each phase
Participate in **Coven Tarot Readings** for valuable insights
Post questions and receive personalized feedback
Simplify your witchcraft, connect with others, and practice more often

Embrace Your Inner Witch
Join this vibrant community and let your magick flow, bringing success
and fulfillment to your life. With comprehensive guidance, support, and exclusive
content, you'll have everything you need to practice witchcraft and thrive.

Your Invitation Awaits

www.witchcraftspellsmagick.com/pages/coven

Contents

Introduction 0
Modern Witchcraft 1

PART 1

Natural Magick 3
Eco Witchcraft 4
Elemental Forces 5
Witches' Sabbats 6
Wheel of the Year 7
Solstices and Equinoxes 8-9
Seasonal Change 10
Seasonal Tracker 11
Foraging and Gathering 12
Witch Supplies 13
Powerful Plants 14
Plant Record 15
Witch's Garden 16
Herb Record 17

PART 2

Divine World 19
Moon Magick 21
2025 Moon Calendar 22
Moon Phases 23
Full Moons 2025 24
Moon Mood Tracker 25
Lunar Magick 26-27
Moon Cookies 28
Baked Magick 29
Astrology 31

Birth Charts 32
Reading a Birth Chart 33
Birth Record 34
Blank Birth Record 35
Planet Rulers 36
Inner Planets 37
Outer Planets / Aspects 38-39
Sun Signs 40
12 Houses 42-43

PART 3

Witchcraft Practices 45
Heart and Hearth 46
Everyday Magick 47
Energy Work 48
Inner Witch 49
Energy Balancing 50
Grounding Ritual 51
A Witch's Altar 52-53
Soulful Ambience 54
Mindful Magick 55
Sacred Space 56
Manifesting 57
Magickal Intent 58
Planning Intentions 59
Ritual 60-61

PART 4
2024 Diary 63
Calendar 65

January 66-89
This Month + Tarot 68-69
Correspondences + Altar 70-71
Month's Witchcraft Practice 72-77
January Weekly 80-89

February 90-111
This Month + Tarot 92-93
Correspondences + Altar 94-95
Month's Practice 96-101
February Weekly 102-111

March 114-136
This Month + Tarot 116-117
Correspondences + Altar 118-119
Month's Practice 120-125
March Weekly 127-136

April 138-158
This Month + Tarot 140-141
Correspondences + Altar 142-143
Month's Practice 144-149
April Weekly 150-158

May 160-181
This Month + Tarot 162-163
Correspondences + Altar 164-165
Month's Practice 166-171
May Weekly 172-181

June 184-206
This Month + Tarot 186-187
Correspondences + Altar 188-189
Month's Practice 190-195
June Weekly 197-206

July 208-228
This Month + Tarot 210-211
Correspondences + Altar 212-213
Month's Practice 214-219
July Weekly 220-228

August 230-251
This Month + Tarot 232-233
Correspondences + Altar 234-235
Month's Practice 236-241
August Weekly 243-251

September 252-272
This Month + Tarot 254-255
Correspondences + Altar 256-257
Month's Practice 258-263
September Weekly 264-272

October 274-295
This Month + Tarot 276-277
Correspondences + Altar 278-279
Month's Practice 280-285
October Weekly 286-295

November 296-317
This Month + Tarot 298-299
Correspondences + Altar 300-301
Month's Practice 302-307
November Weekly 309-317

December 318-338
This Month + Tarot 320-321
Correspondences + Altar 322-323
Month's Practice 324-329
December Weekly 330-338

PART 5
Dream Journal 341-352

Introduction

To All Witches reading this... Welcome!
Witches, are attuned to the energy that flows through everything in the world.

Your magickal abilities can be affected by the noise and stress of modern living, making it difficult to connect with your inner power and the universe's energy.

Some days, your magickal vibrations may feel stronger than others, but it's important to take time to quiet the noise and focus on your craft.

The Practicing Witch Diary is a valuable tool, providing guidance and support for a more engaged approach to practicing witchcraft.

Whether you're seasoned or just starting, this diary helps deepen your connection to the spiritual realm.

Focus your energy and attention, ignite your inner power, and let the magick around you be your journey's guide. Embrace each moment, and watch your magick flourish.

Being a Witch
Modern witches practice witchcraft in various ways, depending on beliefs and traditions. Some perform rituals and spells alone, while others join a coven or group. Your practices may involve meditation, divination, herbalism, and energy work. Cultivate a deep connection with nature and the spiritual realm to manifest positive change in the world.

Incorporate spells into your daily routines, such as stirring a spell into your morning coffee or drawing a protective symbol as you walk through your home. Alternatively, engage in more elaborate rituals with tools, ceremony, and music. Both large and small magickal acts are powerful ways to connect with your spiritual practice and engage the universe's energy.

Ancient Wisdom
Witches have long understood the medicinal properties of plants, using them to alleviate pain and promote energy flow. Witchcraft honors ancestral wisdom and connection to the natural world, emphasizing gratitude, respect for the earth, and ethical harvesting. Practitioners seek to live in balance with the world and cultivate a deeper understanding of the universe's mysteries.

Modern Witchcraft

Modern witchcraft is a spiritual practice that emphasizes a connection with nature and the universe. As a modern witch, you seek to access energies beyond everyday consciousness, including divine, spiritual, and manifesting energies. By identifying with nature and undertaking a journey of self-fulfillment, you are reclaiming the term 'witch' and embracing its empowering connotations. This practice allows you to draw on ancient wisdom while incorporating contemporary elements, making your magick uniquely powerful and relevant in today's world.

Witchcraft Practices

- **Sabbat Celebrations:** Honoring the Wheel of the Year with eight Sabbats—each with unique customs, rituals, and foods reflecting the seasons.
- **Herbal Magick:** Utilizing herbs for healing, protection, and spellwork. Create a magickal garden as a sacred space and source of ingredients.
- **Kitchen Witchery:** Incorporating magick into cooking and baking through chanting, infusing food with intentions, or using herbs with specific correspondences.
- **Folk Magick:** Drawing on regional folklore and practices, including charms, talismans, and local plants in spellwork.

Unique Ideas for Modern Witchcraft

Modern witches innovate and integrate magick into their lives:

- **Techno-Witchcraft:** Using technology to enhance practice, such as digital sigils, apps for moon phases, or online covens.
- **Eco-Witchcraft:** Focusing on sustainability and conservation with eco-friendly spells and earth magick.
- **Artistic Magick:** Channeling creativity into witchcraft through painting, drawing, or writing with hidden spells.
- **Shadow Work:** Delving into the psyche to heal and transform, involving journaling, meditation, and rituals for self-awareness and growth.

Explore these practices, embrace your unique path, and integrate magick into your daily life to unlock your full potential and create positive change.

PART 1

Nature Magick

"Earth my body, Water my blood, Air my breath and Fire my spirit"
Traditional Witchcraft Chant

The term 'Mother Nature' is often used to personify the natural world and its nurturing qualities. It is a reminder that everything you need for your survival and comfort comes from the environment around you, from the food you eat to the materials used to build your home and make your clothes. You rely on nature for your very existence, and it is important to recognize and appreciate the many gifts.

The word 'nature' originated from the Latin word 'natura.' It translates as the forces and events of physical life that are not controlled by humans. Every aspect of nature holds unique energy. Connecting with nature is the first step in welcoming and empowering soul-balancing and healing energy into your magick and everyday life.

The practice of witchcraft is deeply rooted in the natural world, with a reverence for Mother Nature and all her wonders. Witches hold the elements of earth, air, fire, and water as sacred, and honor the cycles of nature, including seasonal changes and the Witches' Sabbats.

Through your connection with the natural world, cultivate a profound sense of peace and harmony with the entire universe.

Guardians of the Earth

Eco-Witchcraft is a spiritual practice that places great emphasis on the natural world and its significance in your daily life.

It acknowledges the vital role that plants play in your existence, providing you with sustenance, healing, and connection to the earth.

Eco-Witches

Eco-Witches harness the energy of nature through spells and rituals, seeking to promote balance and harmony in both your personal life and the world at large.

By cultivating a deep, heartfelt relationship with the environment, Eco-Witches strive to live in harmony with the planet and all its inhabitants.

A World of Plants

The world of plants is full of magick and wonder, but to truly experience it, you must recognize the importance of cultivating a deep connection with nature. This involves opening up your senses to the energy and vibrations of plants, communicating with them on a spiritual level.

Embracing this connection and immersing yourself in the wonder and mystery of nature is the key to unlocking the magickal world of plants. This connection will lead to a deeper understanding of the natural world and a greater sense of harmony with the environment.

Nature Magick

Nature Magick holds power in connecting with nature and its elements, engaging in the spiritual energy that can be harnessed for magickal purposes. Plants have the ability to communicate with you and vice versa. Through touching a plant or tree, you can connect with its energy and receive wisdom and insight. Additionally, plants communicate through energy vibrations, which can be experienced by standing near a plant and trying to connect with it through meditation or visualization. Through these practices, you will access the natural magick of the world around you.

witchcraftspellsmagick.com

Forces of Nature

THE ELEMENTS - Earth, Air, Fire, Water
Balance is essential for your existence and well-being.

Acknowledging and connecting with each of these elemental energies
in a balanced and conscious manner is crucial.
The directions for each element may vary depending on your location.
Listen to your intuition and start with the element
and direction that aligns with you.
By honoring and working with each of the elements,
you will cultivate a deeper connection to the natural world
and enhance your magickal balance and results.

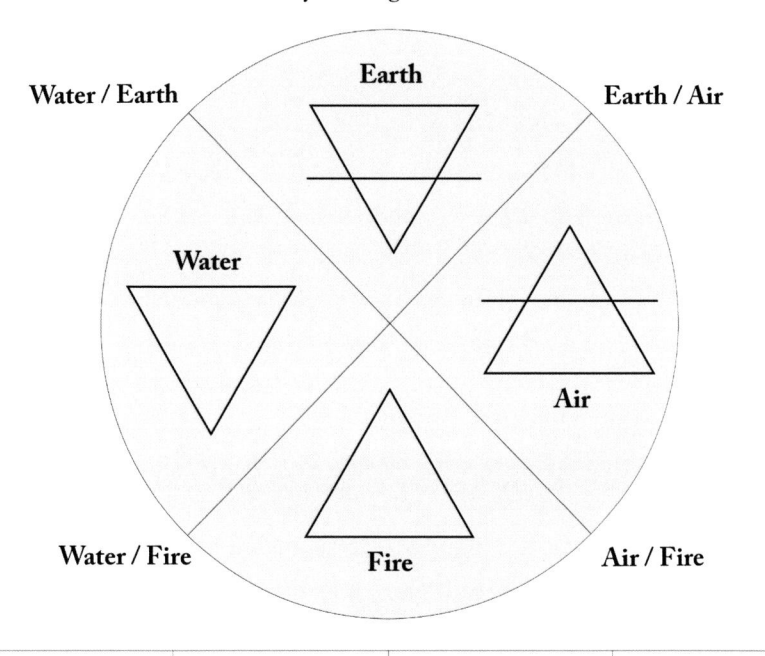

EARTH	AIR	FIRE	WATER
Sustenance for life, your home, where you live, grounding.	Communication, thoughts, wind, inspiration, breath.	Passion, anger, lust, warmth, cooking, survival.	Feelings, emotions, dreams, intuition, friendships.

Witches' Sabbats

Sabbats are a time to let go of what doesn't serve you and engage with positive energy through the ritual cleansing of these sacred festivals. Committing to honoring the 'Pagan Wheel of the Year' is a helpful way to practice witchcraft more regularly and gain more from it.

The Greater Witch Sabbats are sacred festivals celebrated by witches throughout the Wheel of the Year, marking significant points in the seasonal cycle and honoring the rhythms of nature. These Sabbats, including Samhain, Imbolc, Beltane, and Lammas, are times of ritual, celebration, and connection with the divine energies.

The Lesser Witch Sabbats are additional festivals observed by witches, occurring between the Greater Sabbats, marking the equinoxes and solstices. These Sabbats, such as Yule, Ēostre, Litha, and Mabon, serve as important waypoints in the yearly cycle, emphasizing balance, gratitude, and the shifting energies of the natural world.

Wheel of the Year

The Northern and Southern Hemispheres lie in their seasonal patterns, with opposite seasons occurring at the same time due to the tilt of the Earth's axis. While one hemisphere experiences summer, the other experiences winter, resulting in variations in climate, daylight hours, and natural phenomena between the two regions.

IMBOLC Northern: 1 February | Southern: 1 August
SPRING EQUINOX Northern: 20 March | Southern: 23 September
ĒOSTRE (OSTARA) Northern: 19 - 23 March | Southern: 19 - 23 September
BELTANE Northern: 30 April - 1 May | Southern: 31 October - 1 November
SUMMER SOLSTICE Northern: 21 June | Southern: 21 December
LITHA Northern: 21 June | Southern: 21 December
LAMMAS (OR LUGHNASADH) Northern: 1 August | Southern: 1 February
AUTUMN EQUINOX Northern: 22 September | Southern: 20 March
MABON Northern: 22 September | Southern: 20 March
SAMHAIN Northern: 31 October - 1 November | Southern: 30 April - 1 May
WINTER SOLSTICE Northern: 21 December | Southern: 21 June
YULE (YULETIDE) Northern: 21 December - 1 January | Southern: 21 June - 2 July

witchcraftspellsmagick.com

Why do Sabbats matter to Witches?

Sabbats are a powerful time to celebrate and show gratitude to the seasonal and elemental powers that provide you with life. They provide an opportune time for working with divine and metaphysical energies.

Sabbats signify a time to release what no longer serves you and to immerse yourself in positive energy through ritual cleansing. Embracing a commitment to honoring the Pagan Wheel of the Year provides a beneficial framework for practicing witchcraft regularly and gaining greater depth from it.

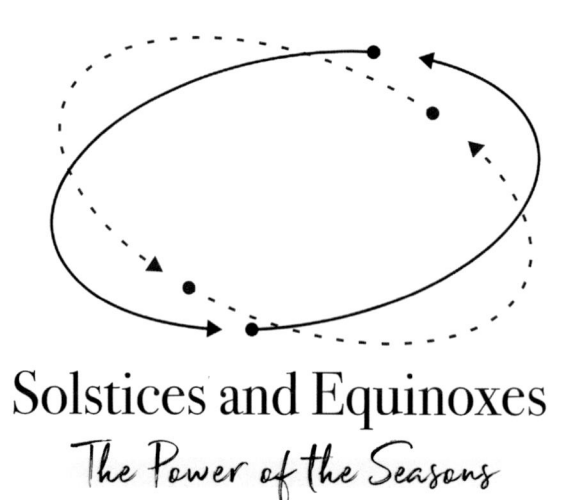

Solstices and Equinoxes
The Power of the Seasons

SPRING VERNAL EQUINOX - March 20, 2025

Spring heralds the awakening of nature, as dormant seeds burst forth with vibrant life and the air fills with the sweet scent of blossoms in bloom. The start of the Spring Equinox marks when day and night are of equal length. Vernal is the Latin word 'ver,' meaning Spring, fresh, and new.

Spring Magick: Intention

With a clear intention in mind, imagine it as a thought-form encapsulated within a seed. Release this thought-form into the fertile soil of your consciousness, allowing it to take root, manifest, and flourish into tangible reality.

SUMMER SOLSTICE - June 21, 2025

The longest day of the year marks the start of the Summer Solstice. With nature's rapid growth through the sustenance of the Summer sun, make sure to be outdoors enjoying nature, celebrating the warmth and vibrancy.

Summer Magick: Manifestation

The intention planted as a seed during Spring now begins to come to fruition. As Summer arrives, you will witness the full bloom and blossoming of your intention into a tangible manifestation.

witchcraftspellsmagick.com

AUTUMN EQUINOX - September 22, 2025

Marking the start of the Autumn Equinox, the day and night are of equal length. Traditionally, this was a time to collect the harvest: grains, seeds, and the last of the season's fruits and vegetables, preserving and storing food for the colder months. The crops and seeds were blessed as harvested, so that the seed would return to the earth until rebirth in Spring, symbolizing the cycle of nature: birth, death, and rebirth.

Autumn Magick: Release

As the leaves descend, carried by the wind's gentle dance, you are reminded of the beauty in letting go. Autumn Magick involves releasing what no longer serves you—shedding old habits, beliefs, and energies to make room for new growth and transformation. Just as trees release their leaves, you too can let go of what weighs you down, entering the new season with renewed lightness and clarity.

WINTER SOLSTICE - December 21, 2025

As the sun reaches its lowest point in the sky, casting long shadows over the land, gather to honor the Winter Solstice. It is a time of reflection, introspection, and renewal. In the darkness, you can find solace, drawing inward to nurture the flame of your inner light. Amidst the cold and stillness, celebrate the promise of rebirth and the return of the light.

Winter Magick: Grounding

In the quiet embrace of winter's chill, you will find grounding and stability. Like the roots of ancient trees reaching deep into the earth, you can anchor yourself in the present moment, finding strength in stillness and silence. Winter Magick is about connecting with the earth, finding solace in nature's rhythms, and grounding yourself in the here and now. As the world slows down around you, you are reminded to pause, to breathe, and to find peace in your existence.

The Solstices and Equinoxes emphasize their roles in the natural cycle and magickal practice, guiding you to align with nature's rhythms and engage the transformative energies of these seasons.

Seasonal Changes
Northern Hemisphere

WINTER SOLSTICE — Earth / North
SPRING EQUINOX — Air / East
SUMMER SOLSTICE — Fire / South
AUTUMN EQUINOX — Water / West

The Wheel of the Year turns through the seasons, each bringing its own unique energies, symbols, and rituals. By aligning with these natural cycles, you will deepen your connection to the elements and enhance your magickal practice. Here is a guide to the key aspects and correspondences for each season:

SPRING EQUINOX	SUMMER SOLSTICE	AUTUMN EQUINOX	WINTER SOLSTICE
Direction: East	**Direction:** South	**Direction:** West	**Direction:** North
Element: Air	**Element:** Fire	**Element:** Water	**Element:** Earth
Tool: Athamé	**Tool:** Candle	**Tool:** Chalice	**Tool:** Pentagram
Sabbat: Ēostre	**Sabbat:** Litha	**Sabbat:** Mabon	**Sabbat:** Yule
Time: Dawn	**Time:** Midday	**Time:** Dusk	**Time:** Midnight
Color: Yellow	**Color:** Red	**Color:** Blue	**Color:** Black

Seasonal Tracker

Take a moment to think and observe the changes that come with each season. Use the table to record relevant information such as average temperatures, daylight hours, upcoming events or holidays, and personal reflections or goals.

This format allows you to systematically monitor and compare seasonal variations, while also encouraging self-reflection on personal experiences and goals throughout the year. Its easy-to-use and practical structure allows for customization based on your individual preferences and needs.

SPRING

Temperature: _____

Weather: _____

Daylight hours: _____

Key seasonal changes: _____
_____

Personal intentions or goals: ____
_____
_____

SUMMER

Temperature: _____

Weather: _____

Daylight hours: _____

Key seasonal changes: _____
_____

Personal intentions or goals: ____
_____
_____

AUTUMN

Temperature: _____

Weather: _____

Daylight hours: _____

Key seasonal changes: _____
_____

Personal intentions or goals: ____
_____
_____

WINTER

Temperature: _____

Weather: _____

Daylight hours: _____

Key seasonal changes: _____
_____

Personal intentions or goals: ____
_____
_____

Foraging and Gathering

Witches savor a deeply unique and obscure interest in what are often termed 'odd' and 'obscure' objects.

Forage and collect gifts from nature: feathers, stones, leaves, and sticks. Acquire found objects, jars, nails, thread, cords, and reuse discarded things found along coastlines, industrial areas, and on nature walks.

To Forage

Witches typically enjoy foraging, which involves looking for and collecting gifts from nature or obscure, odd, unwanted, or discarded objects. Maybe it's the thrill of the find, the energy or magickal potential the object holds, or the visual or tactile pleasure. It is certain and without a doubt that witches feel magick in the objects they find while foraging. The objects may call you, their energy beckoning you—making foraging a magickal act in itself. Always gather with conscious gratitude!

Nature's Treasures

When next you take a walk through a forest, park, beach, or hilltop, collect what you find on your way. Choose a space where you feel grounded, a place that holds positive energy. The word foraging suggests objects are gathered. Branches, for example, should be found, not broken from a tree. Once an object is discovered, pick it up, hold it, and ask yourself: Do I feel a connection? The energy of an object will speak to you, so show gratitude as you gather. Sticks make incredible bases for dream catchers, pentagram crafting, magick wands, altar displays, and many other uses. Add feathers, beads, shells, leaves, and anything that speaks to you. Get creative!

Old Objects Forging

Forage through garage sales, thrift shops, markets, footpaths, or online. Many places hold magickal objects whose power is transferred when chosen, held, or used magickally. Collect found objects, jars, nails, thread, cords, and reuse discarded items. Keep a magickal supplies cupboard ready for your altar practice, spells, witchy crafts, and ritual work.

Inside a Witches' Cupboard

There is a wide variety of enchanting and captivating witch's tools,
many that can easily cost you a small fortune.
Consider an eclectic collection of inexpensive witchy items.

Witchcraft Supplies

Here is a starter list of witchcraft supplies:

Herbs
Herbs must be harvested and dried to be used. Create a list and take advantage of opportunities to stock up.

Flowers
A plant's flower combines beauty, reproduction, and energy, making it ideal for wreaths, altar decorations, or grinding into magick bags and for spell work.

Shells
A symbol of water on your altar, shells offer a calming reminder of the wonders of the natural environment.

Bones, Hair and Teeth
Bones honor a past living creature and should always be held with respect and sacredness. Teeth and hair hold deep connections to where they came from.

Sticks and Wood
Perfect for witchy crafts, besoms, Yule logs, pentagrams, protection, healing, and as an Earth symbol on your altar.

Crystals
Keep them close for extra protection, positive vibes, and calm energy.

Parchment paper
Find in your local art store, this paper burns slowly and emits low smoke.

Sand
Beach Sand - Calms
Desert Sand - Curses
Magnetic Sand - Luck
River Sand - Moving on, Healing
Volcanic Sand - Destruction, Revealing
Black Sand - Protection, Banishing

Seedpods
Perfect for altar decorations and vessels for holding various witchy items.

Cord and Thread
Cords or string in various colors are ideal for a wide range of magickal practices!

Rocks and Stones
Look for those that call to you—sometimes, a stone's energy beckons.

Plant Witchery

Plant witchery is the practice of using plants for their magickal properties, wisdom, and healing abilities.

Plants have been used for centuries in various spiritual and medicinal practices, and their power and energy are still revered today. By embracing eco-consciousness and recognizing the wonders of plants, you can connect with their innate power and enhance your own life.

Powerful Plants

Witches and Plants

Plants have long been an integral part of witchcraft, with witches utilizing their properties in various ways. From cooking to spell work, you can use plants in spell bags, incense, potions, charms, amulets, banishing, healing, cleansing, blessing, protecting, and attracting prosperity and good luck. The list of ways to work with plants is endless and ever-evolving.

Sacred Healing

Sacred healing through the use of plants has been practiced for centuries. Many cultures have recognized the power of plants to heal the body and mind and have used them in traditional medicine. Plants can ease pain, provide relief, and have a profound impact on your overall well-being. As you continue to learn more about the benefits of plants, you will be reminded of the interconnectedness of all living things and the importance of respecting and honoring Mother Nature.

Witch Plant Tips:
Gratitude: Collect only what you need.
Respect: Have a dedicated cutting board, knife, mortar, and pestle for preparation.
Sacred: Consciously bundle and dry upside down.
Honor: Mindfully combine with intent.

witchcraftspellsmagick.com

Plant Record

Keeping a plant journal is a great way to deepen your knowledge and connection with plant magick and energy in your witchcraft practice.

In your journal, you can include information on the properties and uses of different plants, as well as your personal experiences and observations when working with them. The more you learn and document, the more you can draw on this knowledge to enhance your spells and rituals.

Sketch the Plant

Name of Plant: _____ **Date:** _____

Description / Characteristics: _____

_____

Warnings / Toxicity: _____

_____

Medicinal Use: _____

_____

Magickal Use: _____

_____

Observations: _____

_____

Witch's Garden

Growing your own herbs offers a fulfilling way to connect with nature's magick.

Whether from your own garden or found in the wild, each herb carries its own unique energy. Harvest with care and intention, or cultivate wild herbs with gratitude. Below are a few magickal herbs to start up your Witch's Garden!

ALYSSUM
Peace, spiritual, calm, moderation, emotional balance.

MARIGOLD
Protection, solar influence, consecration.

SAGE
Purification, protection, wisdom, health.

CATNIP
Peace, happiness, good fortune, protection.

MUGWORT
Divination, dreams, peace, banishing.

SKULLCAP
Peace to a chaotic environment, calms disruption.

CHAMOMILE
Protect, bless, medicinal healing power.

PARSLEY
Power, strength, purification, prosperity.

THYME
Aligned with Jupiter, ideal to invoke energies.

EVENING PRIMROSE
Love, vitality, lunar work, good fortune.

PENNYROYAL
Enhances strength, protection, peace, and clarity.

VERVAIN
Creative visions, good for all magick.

LAVENDER
Psychic, visionary work, dreams, sleep, meditation, calm.

ROSEMARY
Protection, memory, wisdom, purification.

WORMWOOD
Divination, purify, protect, banish negative.

MILK THISTLE
Breaking negativity, healing, strength.

RUE
Powerful purifications, protection, banish.

YARROW
Love, relationships, connections, wellbeing.

witchcraftspellsmagick.com

Herb Record

Keeping a herb journal is a more niche version of a plant journal, which might suit you better. Journaling will deepen your knowledge and connection with herb magick and energy.

Include information on the properties and uses of different herbs, along with your personal experiences and observations. The more you learn and document, the more you can draw on this knowledge to enhance your spells and rituals.

Sketch the Herb

Name of Herb: _____ **Date:** _____

Description / Characteristics: _____

_____

Warnings / Toxicity: _____

_____

Medicinal Use: _____

_____

Magickal Use: _____

_____

Observations: _____

_____

PART 2
Divine World

"As above, so below; As below, so above"
The Kybalion

Originating from the ancient Hermetic text known as the 'Emerald Tablet,'
attributed to Hermes Trismegistus, likely around 600 CE,
this phrase is a foundational principle in Hermeticism
and has influenced various philosophical and esoteric traditions.
The Universe is a source of wisdom and knowledge for those who seek it.
Witches know that the energy from celestial bodies such as the moon, planets,
and stars can guide them in their daily, monthly, and yearly practices.

This knowledge is based on the principle of correspondence,
which states that there is a connection between the laws
and phenomena of different planes of existence.
The Hermetic axiom "As above, so below; as below, so above"
reflects this principle.
By understanding the laws of correspondence, you will bridge the gap
between the material, mental, and spiritual planes, making universal knowledge
and Hermetic understanding valuable tools in your practice of magick.

Recommended Reading:
Hermes Trismegistus. 'The Corpus Hermeticum'.
Agrippa, Heinrich Cornelius. 'Three Books of Occult Philosophy'.
'The Kybalion by Three Initiates'.
Bardon, Franz. 'Initiation into Hermetics'.

Moon Magick
The Charge of the Goddess
by Doreen Valiente

"Listen to the words of the Great Mother,
who of old was also called Artemis; Astarte; Diana; Melusine; Aphrodite;
Cerridwen; Dana; Arianrhod; Isis; Bride; and by many other names.

Whenever ye have need of anything, once in a month,
and better it be when the Moon be full, then ye shall assemble
in some secret place and adore the spirit of me, who am Queen of all Witcheries.

There shall ye assemble, ye who are fain to learn all sorcery,
yet have not yet won its deepest secrets:
to these will I teach things that are yet unknown."

For the full poem and copyright, visit www.doreenvaliente.com

2025 Moon Calendar

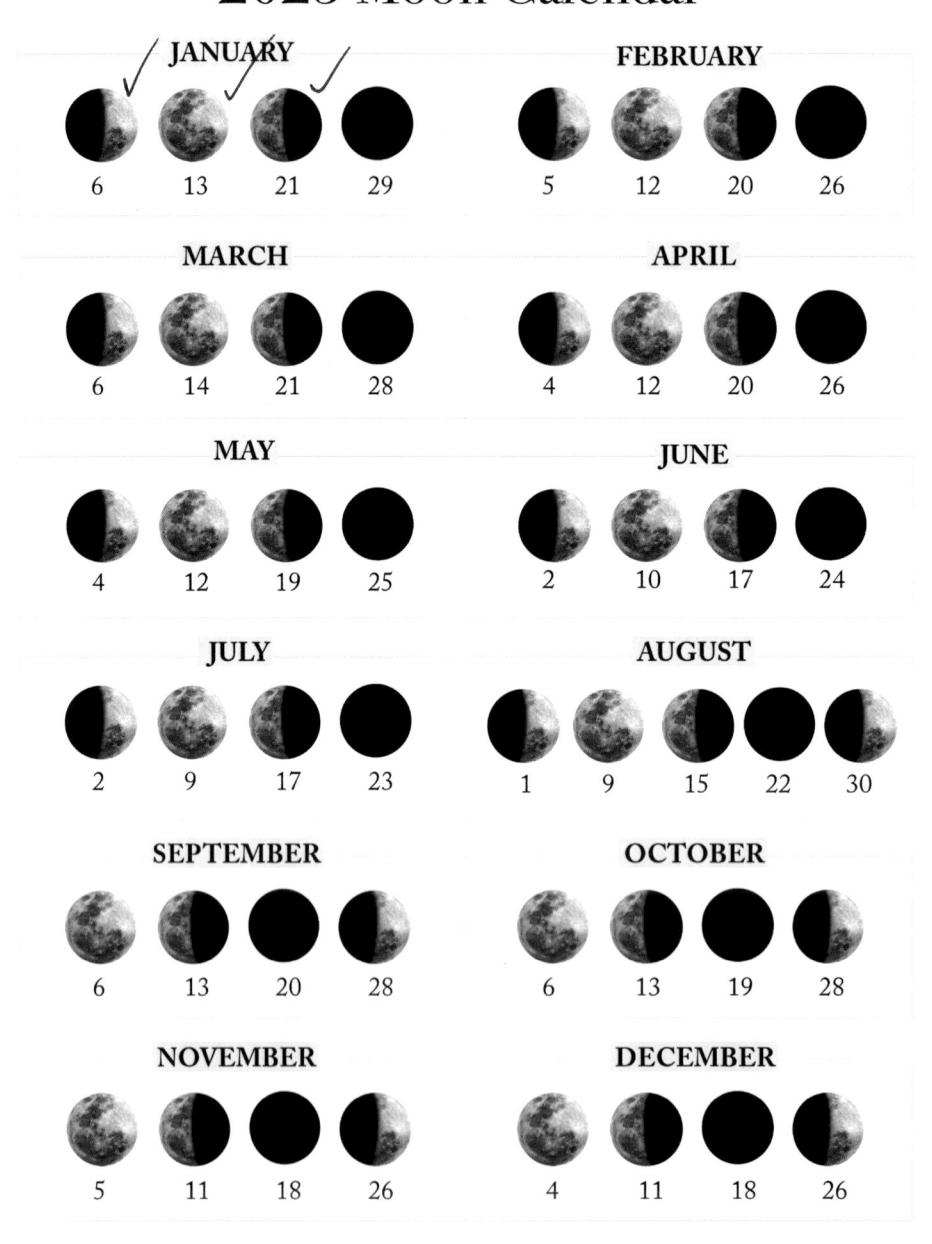

JANUARY
6   13   21   29

FEBRUARY
5   12   20   26

MARCH
6   14   21   28

APRIL
4   12   20   26

MAY
4   12   19   25

JUNE
2   10   17   24

JULY
2   9   17   23

AUGUST
1   9   15   22   30

SEPTEMBER
6   13   20   28

OCTOBER
6   13   19   28

NOVEMBER
5   11   18   26

DECEMBER
4   11   18   26

These dates have been confirmed as an average for the Northern Hemisphere from multiple sources, including Calendar-12, FullMoonology, Moonphase.info, and Timeanddate.com.

witchcraftspellsmagick.com

2025 Book of Shadows   23

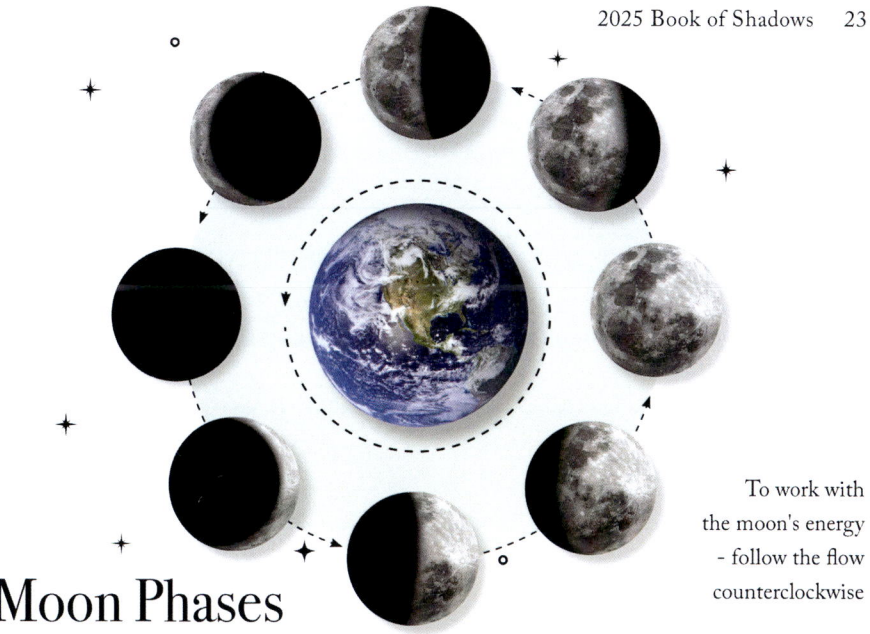

Moon Phases

To work with the moon's energy - follow the flow counterclockwise

Engage the power of the Moon's energy during each lunar cycle.

DARK MOON or New Moon	WAXING CRESCENT MOON	FIRST QUARTER MOON	WAXING GIBBOUS MOON
Dark stillness, with a gleam of the new moon. Change, rebirth, and manifestation. **Cycle Phases:** New beginnings, set goals.	The gleam grows, offering a reset and refresh. **Cycle Phases:** Nurture your ideas, intentions, and goals.	A distinct luminosity lights the sky. Attracting ideas with balance. **Cycle Phases:** Take action and apply your ideas.	Shining brighter, leading to the Full Moon. **Cycle Phases:** Growth, idea evolution, goals, and intentions.
FULL MOON Illuminating the night sky with complete lunar energy. Optimal for intuitive, divination, and sensory magick. **Cycle Phases:** Bringing intentions and ideas to life.	**WANING GIBBOUS MOON** As the lustre retreats, eliminate obstacles and shape outcomes. **Cycle Phases:** Clarity to what no longer aligns.	**LAST QUARTER MOON** Rise above challenges and surrender as the moon's luminosity diminishes. **Cycle Phases:** Detox anything holding back your ideas.	**WANING CRESCENT MOON** Spiritual calm and balanced energy. **Cycle Phases:** The cycle is completed. Reseed ideas, intentions, and goals, if required.

Full Moons 2025

Journey through the lunar year, unlocking lunar insights.
Exploring the Full Moon's influence in each Moon Sign.

JANUARY 13, 2025
Full Moon in Cancer
Energies: Creative, warm-hearted, inflexible.

FEBRUARY 12, 2025
Full Moon in Leo
Energies: Creative, warm-hearted, inflexible.

MARCH 14, 2025
Full Moon in Virgo
Energies: Analytical, insightful, anxious.

APRIL 12, 2025
Micro Full Moon in Libra
Energies: Cooperative, gracious, critical.

MAY 12, 2025
Micro Full Moon in Scorpio
Energies: Secretive, manipulative, dramatic.

JUNE 10, 2025
Full Moon in Sagittarius
Energies: Generous, intelligent, impatient.

JULY 9, 2025
Full Moon in Capricorn
Energies: Disciplined, analytical, selfish.

AUGUST 9, 2025
Full Moon in Aquarius
Energies: Humanitarian, tolerance, moody.

SEPTEMBER 6, 2025
Full Moon in Pisces
Energies: Artistic, intuitive, indecisive.

OCTOBER 6, 2025
Full Moon in Aries
Energies: Determine, impatience, aggressive.

NOVEMBER 5, 2025
Super Full Moon in Taurus
Energies: Reliable, practical, stubborn.

DECEMBER 4, 2025
Super Full Moon in Gemini
Energies: Friendly, gentle, indecisive.

In 2025, there will be a total of 12 full moons, with a lunar eclipse in March and Micro Moons in April and May, as well as Super Full Moons in November and December. Full moon dates are determined using information from timeanddate.com, mooncalendar.com, and NASA. Please cross-check these references to determine the precise time and date according to your geographic location.

witchcraftspellsmagick.com

Moon Mood Tracker

Explore the profound connection between moon phases and your energy for enhanced intuition and personal growth.

Keep track of your emotions and feelings during different moon phases to optimize and support your daily life.

Moon Phase	**Moods**
1. Dark Moon / New Moon	A. Amazing
2. Waxing Crescent Moon	G. Good
3. First Quarter	P. Productive
4. Waxing Gibbous Moon	S. So-So
5. Full Moon	R. Relaxed
6. Waning Gibbous Moon	E. Exhausted
7. Last Quarter Moon	O. Overwhelmed
8. Waning Cresent Moon	D. Defeated

Months

Moon Phase	J	F	M	A	M	J	J	A	S	O	N	D
1												
2												
3												
4												
5												
6												
7												
8												

Lunar Magick

**Manifest new ideas during the Dark or New Moon phases
and bring them into tangible existence through the lunar cycle.**

Connecting deeply with each lunar cycle is a potent and transformative experience for both you and your magickal practice.

DARK MOON | NEW MOON:
Intentional Magick

Write down your intentions for the new lunar cycle. Keep the intentions succinct; if they're too complex, spells may become muddled.

Lunar intention ideas:
Love, good fortune, gratitude, foresight,
or banishment of something from your life.

Magickal method:
Light a candle and whisper your intentions
(focus on one intention at a time) towards the flickering flame.

Concentrate on the flame, repeating your intention in sets of three.
Three is the magickal number, representing growth, communication, sharing, and nurturing. You might like to move your hands from either side of the flame outwards, drawing energy from the flame. Blow out the candle, then push your hands down to the earth, grounding and seeding your intention in preparation to manifest.

Your moon magick journey has commenced; maintain the vitality of your intention throughout the lunar cycle by consistently practicing this ritual. Repeat your seeded intention as often as you can remember to do so throughout the day, before sleep, while walking, etc. Repeat, repeat, repeat! If you wrote down your intention and can now remember it, burn, bury, or soak the paper in moon water. As you do this, visualize your intention coming to fruition and manifesting in your life.

witchcraftspellsmagick.com

WAXING MOON
Imitative Magick

Continue to manifest and visualize your intention for the lunar cycle.
Act out, mimic, describe in detail, draw, or create in clay
exactly how your goal or intention can become tangible
- this is 'Imitative Magick', the Law of Similarity.

FULL MOON
Mindful Blessings

When the moon is full, give extra potency to your bath or shower.
Use essential oils or flower petals such as roses, marigold, or chamomile,
or a mix. Gently pat the petals on your skin, inhale the aroma, and mindfully
bless each part of your body. Breathe deeply and surrender to self-kindness.
Feel the full moon shining bright and allow your entire inner self to be illuminated
with her energy. Afterwards, scatter the flower petals under the full moon.

WANING MOON
Banishment Spell

Write down what you need to banish. Light a candle and focus on the flame,
saying, 'I banish... (name of person, energy, or situation) from my being - be gone,'
and repeat three times. Carefully burn the paper, visualizing what you have banished
leaving your being. Collect and bury or scatter the ashes in the wind.
Blow out the candle with intent.

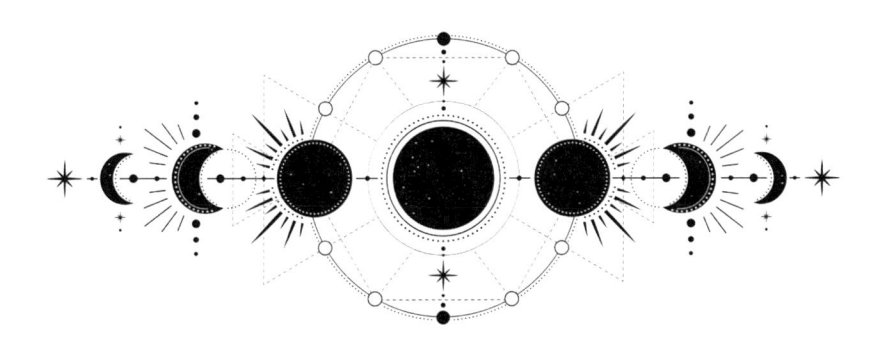

Moon Cookies

The purpose of moon cookies is to serve as an offering in your magickal practice and aid in grounding when consumed afterward.

SHORTBREAD RECIPE

Preparation time: 15 minutes
Baking time: 12 minutes

INGREDIENTS:

2 cups coconut flour
1/4 cup coconut sugar
1/2 cup (100g) butter or vegan alternative
1/2 tsp vanilla extract

METHOD:

Step 1: Preheat the oven to 325°F or 160 °C lining your baking tray with unbleached brown baking paper.

Step 2: In a mixing bowl, combine the coconut flour and coconut sugar.

Step 3: Next add the softened vegan butter and vanilla extract. Mix with a wooden spoon or on the low speed of an electric mixer until mixed well. The dough will look crumbly, soft and easily squash together with your hands.

Step 4: Place a sheet of brown baking paper on your kitchen top and sprinkle with a little flour.

Step 5: Form a dough ball with the mixture and place on the brown baking paper. Add another sprinkle of flour and another sheet of baking paper on top, so the dough is in the middle.

Step 6: Roll the dough to an even 1/2 inch (1.25 cm) thickness.

Step 7: Remove the paper and cut your moon cookies. Use a moon-shaped cookie cutter or a sharp knife. Alternatively, a nice little trick is to use a circle from a glass, pushing down to create full moons. Then move the glass over to cut out crescent moons - depending on the current moon cycle.

Step 8: Continue re-forming and rolling the dough until it is all used.

Step 9: Bake in the oven for 12 minutes, until slightly golden.

Step 10: Let cool for 5-10 minutes before cooling on a baking rack.

Step 11: Store in an airtight container for 5-6 days.

Extra magickal ingredients on next page.

witchcraftspellsmagick.com

Baked Magick

Grounding after performing a witchcraft spell or ritual is important to rebalance your energy. One way to do this is by nourishing your body with food.

Baked magick, in particular, can be a powerful way to receive the benefits of the potion you created during your practice. Remember to approach food with gratitude and appreciation for the sustenance it provides for your life.

Why Consume Magickal Offerings? Consuming magickal offerings is a way to connect with the energies you worked with during spellwork. Consuming homemade offerings infused with your intentions strengthens your connection to the divine, metaphysical, and elemental energies you work with.

Gratitude and Reflection

Baking an offering is an ideal way to show gratitude to a deity, spirit, ancestor, or totem animal in your altar and in your magickal practice.

MAGICKAL INGREDIENTS

These ingredients are best added one by one and taste tested.

All are available from your grocer, but try home-growing when possible!

Love - Rosemary, Caraway seeds, or Honey
Prosperity - Cinnamon, Nutmeg, Basil, or Lemon
Health - Carob, Chamomile, or Chia seeds
Intuition - Celery seeds, Marshmallow root, or Acacia powder
Calm - Cacao, Lavender, or Anise seeds
Psychic and Divination - Orange, Thyme, or Nutmeg
Protection - Cloves, Aniseed, or a pinch of Salt
Good Fortune - Catnip, Juniper, or Poppy seeds
Career and Work - Elderberry, Ginger, or Oats
Hexing - Capsicum powder, Paprika, or Chilli powder
Reverse Negativity - Clove, Thyme, or Elderberry

Astrology

Your ancestors viewed the planets and stars as ruling beings, guiding various aspects of your lives.

Embrace the wisdom of Ancient Astrology to navigate modern life with insight and understanding. This ancient science offers invaluable guidance for navigating the complexities of modern life.

Planets
Aspects
'What'

Sun
Signs
'How'

Houses
'Where'

Planets - The celestial bodies interpret aspects of personality, behavior, and life events. This section delves into the identification of astrological influences, focusing on 'What' they represent.

Zodiac Signs - Focuses on interpreting the signs of the zodiac associated with the Sun, providing practical guidance on their application. This section explains 'How' to utilize information from the Planets section effectively.

Houses - Represent the twelve sectors in your astrological chart. This section guides you on 'Where' to find astrological insights in your life.

Birth Charts

What is a Birth Chart?

Your birth chart is a snapshot of the celestial alignment at the moment of your birth. It captures the positions of the moon, planets, and stars, providing a unique cosmic blueprint that shapes your personality and life path.

What is a Birth Chart used for?

Birth charts serve as invaluable tools for understanding yourself. They illuminate how you process information, experience love, navigate turbulent times, approach work, and harness your energy. Understanding astrology's influence on your life is a valuable skill that guides you through areas needing extra attention, as well as highlighting your strengths and weaknesses.

It's crucial to know the exact time of your birth for some results, though not all. Without this information, creating a complete birth chart is impossible. However, even with partial data, you can obtain helpful insights to guide you. Instead of relying on guesswork, it's best to work with the known facts to avoid misleading interpretations.

Access a Free Birth Chart!
cafeastrology.com

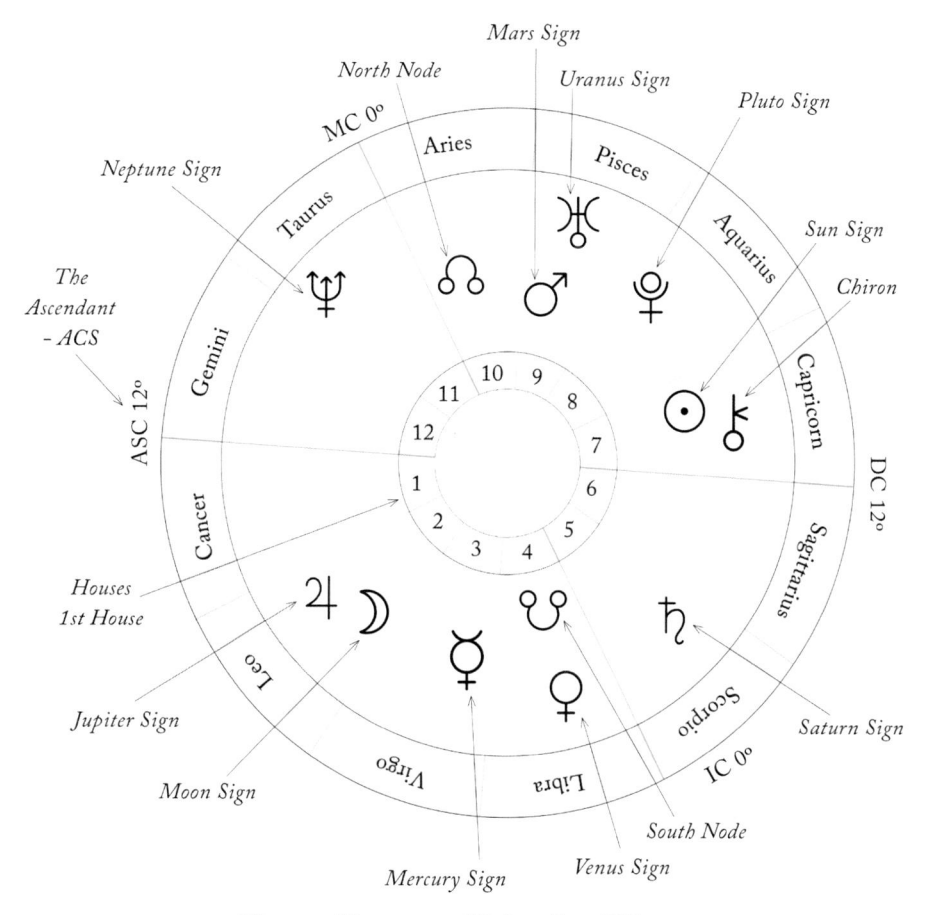

Reading a Birth Chart
Understanding the Structure of a Birth Chart

A Birth Chart is an intricate map of the heavens at the moment of your birth, revealing a wealth of insights into your character, life path, and potential. This chart provides a guide to understanding the various symbols and their meanings in astrology.

Activity in the **Upper Hemisphere** of the chart refers to your **Public Life.**
Activity in the **Lower Hemisphere** is your **Private Life.**
Activity in the **Left** signifies **Freedom,** while activity in the **Right** denotes **Fate.**
Further pages explain each sign in detail.

Birth Record

Your birth chart, also known as a natal chart, provides a snapshot of the positions of celestial bodies at the exact moment of your birth.

By documenting your birth record and understanding these alignments, you can gain valuable insights into your personality, strengths, challenges, and life path.

Complete the section below with the cosmic alignment present during your birth, as this will offer valuable insight into your astrological profile and provide a deeper understanding of your personality traits and life path.

☉	**Sun** _____
☽	**Moon** _____
ASC 12°	**Ascendant	ASC** _____
DC 12°	**Descendant	DES** _____
MC 0°	**Mid Heaven	MC** _____
IC 0°	**Imum Coeli	IC** _____
☿	**Mercury** _____
♀	**Venus** _____
♂	**Mars** _____
♃	**Jupiter** _____
♄	**Saturn** _____
♅	**Uranus** _____
♆	**Neptune** _____
♇	**Pluto** _____
☊	**North Node** _____
☋	**South Node** _____
⚷	**Chiron** _____

witchcraftspellsmagick.com

2025 Book of Shadows   35

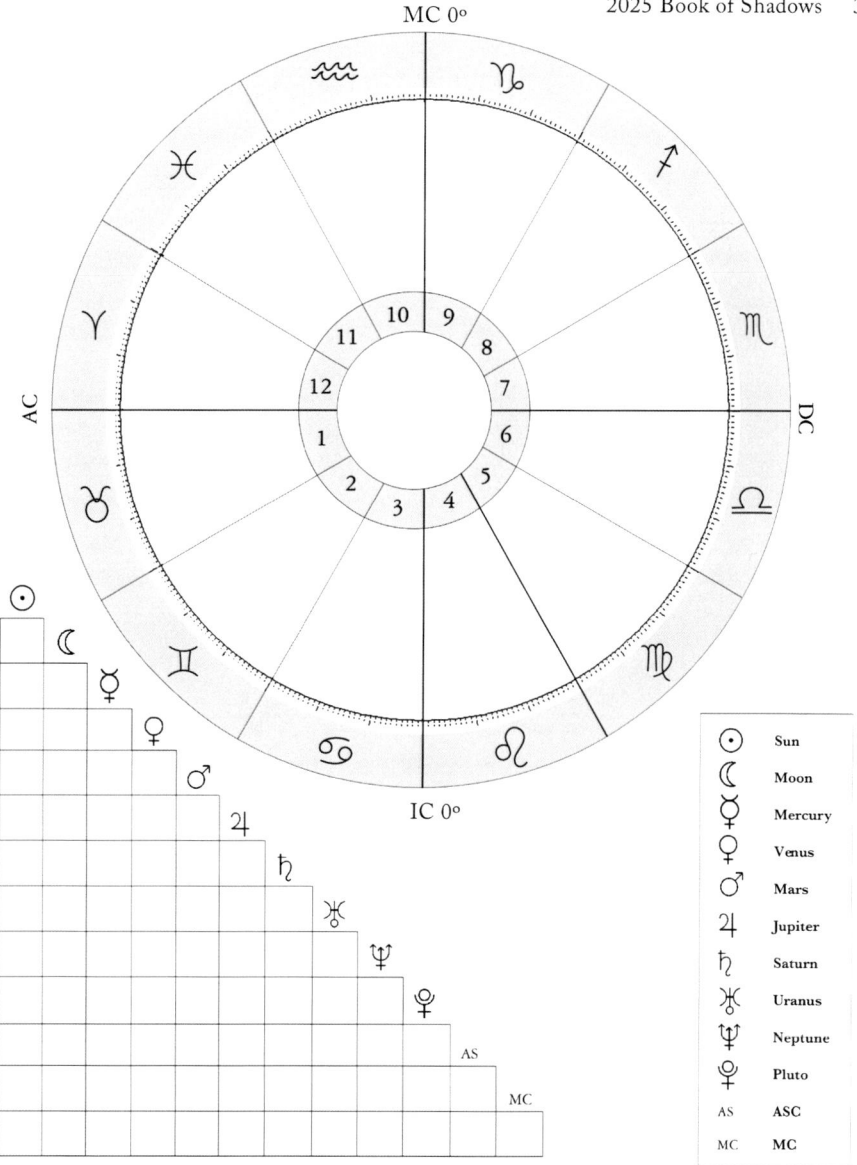

☉	Sun
☾	Moon
☿	Mercury
♀	Venus
♂	Mars
♃	Jupiter
♄	Saturn
♅	Uranus
♆	Neptune
♇	Pluto
AS	ASC
MC	MC

Blank Birth Chart

Instructions: Identify your planetary positions and the houses they occupy based on your birth information. Mark the positions of your planets in the corresponding house sections. Draw lines between planets to indicate major aspects (e.g., conjunctions, trines, squares). Use the aspect grid to note the aspects between each planet.

Planet Rulers

The planet rulers were in a particular alignment when you were born, forming your Birth Chart.

The Inner Planets include the Sun, Moon, Mercury, Venus, and Mars.
Other aspects to consider are the Ascendant and Midheaven.
The Outer Planets consist of Jupiter, Saturn, Uranus, Neptune, and Pluto.

Where to start?

The Primal Triad

Understanding too many alignments can be overwhelming.
**Focus on the three dominant signs in your birth chart:
your Sun, Moon, and Ascendant (or Rising Sign)**

Inner Planets

To access your birth chart, you will need a few things: your birth date, location, and time. If you don't know the time of your birth, you can still work with the information you have.

Focusing on the positions of the inner planets—the Sun, Moon, Mercury, Venus, and Mars—provides valuable insights into your personality, emotions, communication style, relationships, and basic drives and desires. Analyzing the positions of these inner planets and exploring the interactions between them and their aspects can deepen your understanding of yourself and your astrological makeup.

Sun Self - Your Ego

Associations: Sunday, Numbers 1 and 8, Gold, Brass, Citrine, Diamonds, Amber, Mistletoe, Almond, Angelica, Chamomile. Your Sun Sign represents your unique identity and personality, embodying your inner spark and spirit, the core of who you are.

Moon - Your Emotions

Associations: Monday, Number 2, Silver, Pearls, Opal, Moonstone. Encapsulates your emotional needs, instincts, sensitivities, intuition, mood, and subconscious. Your Moon Sign holds answers and guidance to what makes you happy and fulfilled.

Ascendant Rising sign - First Impressions

The (ASC) marks the eastern horizon at your birth and represents your image to the world and how you present yourself.

Mercury - Communication

Associations: Wednesday, Yellow, Aquamarine, Lavender, Peppermint. Mercury's energy represents how you communicate, your daily expression, and how you work through problems, information, and ideas.

Venus - Love

Associations: Friday, Copper, Bronze, Emerald, Rose Quartz, Sapphire. Venus is the planet of love, sensuality, comforts, social graces, beauty, creativity, and harmonious relationships, making Venus central to matters of the heart.

Mars - Aggression + Instinct

Associations: Tuesday, Iron, Brass, Bloodstone, Magnetite, Ruby, Hematite. Mars represents our primitive urges, innate energy, anger, self-preservation, rage, passion, and lust.

Outer Planets + Aspects

In astrology, the outer planets play a significant role in defining your subconscious and the hidden aspects of yourself.

When the outer planets form aspects with the inner planets in your birth chart, it can reveal insights into your deeper self that may not be immediately apparent in your daily life. These planetary interactions can help you access and understand the depths of your psyche.

♃ Jupiter - Success

Associations: *Thursday, #3, Tin, Sapphire, Topaz, Oak Tree.*

Jupiter is your driving force to expand and succeed. A strong Jupiterian influence in your birth chart signifies a propensity for growth, abundance, and a steadfast belief in the power of optimism to manifest success in various aspects of life. It indicates a cheerful, optimistic disposition, good energy, striving to surpass expectations and approach life's challenges with positivity and resilience.

♄ Saturn - Authority

Associations: *Saturday, #4, Lead, Iron, Steel, Diamond, Onyx.*

How you live by your moral and ethical values. Saturn guides our life's journey and quest. Saturn's influence challenges boundaries and limitations, shaping your fate and guiding our destinies. This planet demands discipline and responsibility, encouraging growth through trials and perseverance. Additionally, Saturn influences your fate, willpower, and the outcomes you are destined to experience.

witchcraftspellsmagick.com

⛢ Uranus - Humanity
Associations: *Wednesday, #4, Uranium, Aquamarine.*

Uranus represents your connection to the divine and the humanity of your soul. It contains energy that belongs to your spirit and is associated with innovation and sudden change, often leading to groundbreaking ideas and insights.

♆ Neptune - Creativity
Associations: *#7, Amethyst, Jade, Coral, Aquamarine.*

Neptune represents your link between the spiritual and material worlds. It encompasses the three depths of consciousness: unconscious, conscious, and cosmic consciousness. This planet engages in the deepest levels of illusion, ranging from profound spiritual insights to the depths of delusion and deception.

♇ Pluto - Resilience
Associations: *Persephone, Jet, Smoky Quartz, Obsidian.*

Pluto symbolizes how you demonstrate regeneration and resilience, allowing you to withstand the deepest and darkest parts of your psyche. It deals with emotional toxicity and transformation, where energy stored within can be released with Pluto's intense and transformative vibrations.

Aspects

Aspects refer to the angles and degrees between planets in the zodiac. These relationships are represented by lines on a birth chart, creating a complex web of energies.

By analyzing these aspects, you can gain insight into personality traits, strengths, and challenges, enabling you to make the most of your unique talents and abilities.

THE MOON'S NODES

North Node - Life's Path

The North Node tells of your life's journey, your soul's purpose, destiny, and fate.

South Node - The Past

The South Node presents a challenge: carry from the past only that which serves you, leaving the negative where it belongs - behind you.

ASTROID

Chiron - The Wounded Healer

The most recent astrological addition, both warrior and healer. This explains why you are hurting and where to heal.

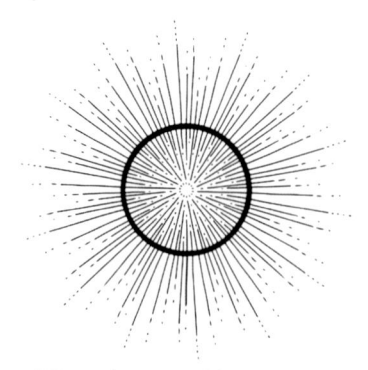

Zodiac Signs

The 12 Zodiac Sun Signs represent distinct astrological personalities based on the position of the sun at the time of your birth.

The spring equinox on March 21 marks the beginning of the new zodiac year for the Northern Hemisphere, with Aries initiating the cycle. If you are born on a cusp, refer to the year you were born for clarification of your sign.

Aquarius
Water Bearer: Jan 20 – Feb 18
Expressive, Thoughtful, and Enthusiastic
Energy: Saturn and Uranus, **Air sign**
Represents: Peaceful, friendly, humble, eccentric, and occasional confusion.

Pisces
Fish: Feb 19 – March 20
Dreams and Psychic work
Energy: Jupiter, Neptune, **Water sign**
Represents: Offers very powerful past-life energy and can find things potent.

Aries
Ram: March 21 – April 19
Headstrong and Enthusiastic
Energy: Mars, **Fire sign**
Represents: Fiery emotions, strengths, daring, aggression, quick wins, and power.

Taurus
Bull: April 20 – May 20
Love and the Arts
Energy: Venus, **Earth sign**
Represents: Values, creative arts, sensuality, hard work, caution, and stubbornness.

Gemini
Twins: May 21 – June 20
Strength in Dual
Energy: Mercury, **Air sign**
Represents: Juggling, balanced mostly, at times uncertain.

Cancer
Crab: June 21 – July 22
Emotions and Nurturing
Energy: The Moon, **Water sign**
Represents: Mother-child dynamics, nurturing emotions, and seeding ideas.

witchcraftspellsmagick.com

♌ Leo
Lion: July 23 – Aug 22
Positive and Strong
Energy: The Sun, **Fire sign**
Represents: Strength in action, positivity, loyalty, and kindness.

♍ Virgo
Virgin: Aug 23 – Sept 22
Abstract and Critical Thought
Energy: Mercury, **Earth sign**
Represents: often seen as critical due to their meticulous nature and organizational skills

♎ Libra
Balance: Sept 23 – Oct 22
Balancing Accomplishments
Energy: Venus, **Air sign**
Represents: Partnerships, legality, social ties, and equilibrium.

♏ Scorpio
Scorpion: Oct 23 – Nov 21
Occult and Hidden Elements
Energy: Mars and Pluto, **Water sign**
Represents: Emotions that can morph into obsession, occasionally very self-centered.

♐ Sagittarius
Archer: Nov 22 – Dec 21
Warmhearted and Friendly
Energy: Jupiter, **Fire sign**
Represents: Bold, enjoys both company and solitude, adaptable, and playful.

♑ Capricorn
Goat: Dec 22 – Jan 19
Wise and Autocratic Manner
Energy: Saturn, **Earth sign**
Represents: Profound, talented, prone to ruthless behavior, wise in many ways.

Elemental Energies

Fire signs embody passion, Earth signs symbolize stability, Air signs represent intellect, and Water signs symbolize emotions.

Elemental energies linked to each zodiac sign offer profound insights into core traits. Understanding these influences aids in navigating your life's challenges and embracing strengths and weaknesses.

EARTH SIGNS
Taurus, Virgo, Capricorn
Sensuality, practicality, stubbornness, endurance, reliability.

AIR SIGNS
Gemini, Libra, Aquarius
Thoughts, ideas, inspiration, strife, conflict.

FIRE SIGNS
Aries, Leo, Sagittarius
Assertiveness, passion, lust, anger, daring, and unyielding drive.

WATER SIGNS
Cancer, Scorpio, Pisces
Emotion, feelings, intuition, dreams, desires, pleasure, friendship, social.

The Astro Houses and Angles

Your birth chart reading starts with the ascendant. Proceeding counter-clockwise through each house in turn. At the ascendant, your soul is incarnated and commences expressing your identity. Moving through the houses and undergoing cosmic programming.

Angles

At the ascendant (ASC), your soul is incarnated and commences expressing your identity.

RISING ASCENDANT | RISING OR ASC

Rising marks the Eastern horizon at the moment of your birth. Your image or face to the world, how you present to others. This is your first impression, how the world sees you at face value.

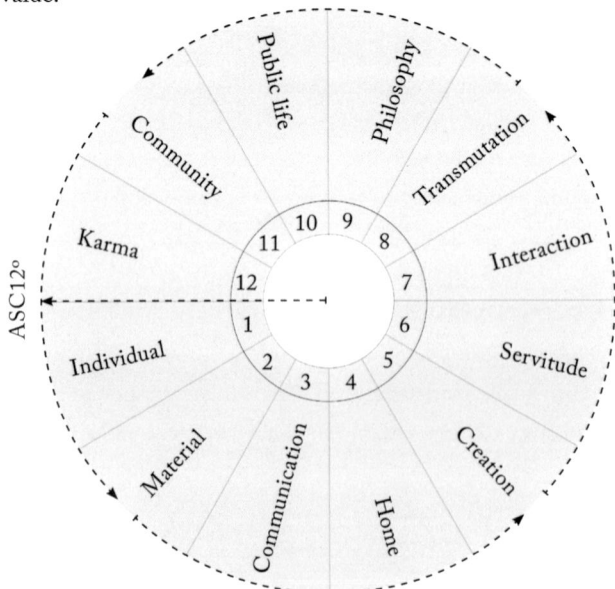

DESCENDANT, DES	MID HEAVEN, MC	IMUM COELI, IC
Descendant marks the Western horizon at the moment of your birth.	Midheaven marks the highest point the sun traverses on your chart.	Imum Coeli, is Latin for 'bottom of the sky,' the opposite point to MC.

witchcraftspellsmagick.com

Houses

Divided into 12 different sections on your birth chart are the Houses. Each one represents a different aspect of your cosmic programming. Houses should be read starting with the Ascendant or ASC and read counter clock wise or moon-wise on your birth chart. Identifiability self, expression, childhood, adulthood, work, play, friends, positive, negative, intimacy, and community.

FIRST HOUSE
1. Individuality
Birth and childhood experiences shape your initial identity and personality.

SECOND HOUSE
2. Resources + Possessions
Ownership of material possessions contributes to a psychological sense of self-worth.

THIRD HOUSE
3. Communication
This house governs rational expression and how you convey our thoughts.

FOURTH HOUSE
4. Home
Represents our emotional foundation, providing security and protection.

FIFTH HOUSE
5. Creation
Creativity in various forms, such as music, ideas, and dreams, reflects your soul's essence.

SIXTH HOUSE
6. Servitude
Defines how you utilize your talents and strengths to serve and share knowledge with others.

SEVENTH HOUSE
7. Interaction
Balances personal needs within relationships and partnerships.

EIGHTH HOUSE
8. Transmutation
Involves the exchange and transformation of self-love, consciousness, and universal awareness.

NINTH HOUSE
9. Philosophy
Explores deeper existential questions and higher learning beyond the mundane.

TENTH HOUSE
10. Outer Environment
Reflects your ambitions, aspirations, and how you leave your mark on the world.

ELEVENTH HOUSE
11. Community
Defines your place within societal groups or communities, expressing personal identity through collective affiliation.

TWELFTH HOUSE
12. Karma
Represents past experiences, including karma and unconscious behaviors that shape present circumstances.

PART 3
Witchcraft Practices

The Craft of the Wise

*The term 'Craft of the Wise' originated with Robert Cochrane,
although Doreen Valiente also utilized it in her books.*

Witchcraft practices are considered the oldest spiritual traditions in human history, dating back to the beginning of humanity.
These practices involve accessing a deep-rooted and innate spirituality, with witches embarking on lifelong personal journeys toward self-discovery and enlightenment. Witchcraft utilizes spells, rituals, and other means, offering practitioners a unique and powerful way to connect with the spiritual world.

Witchcraft practices involve effectively communing with your intuition, achieved through various meditation techniques, energy work, and mindful magick. It's important to explore your intentions and plan your magick with purpose in order to manifest powerful energies that can shift, change, and transform the surrounding energies. These practices have evolved over time, with modern witches incorporating various rituals and spells into their daily lives. Strive to act consciously and walk with intention, embracing your close friendship with nature.

Immerse yourself in the world of witchcraft by creating a sacred space and setting up monthly altars. Connect with the practices of your ancient ancestors and explore primal ritual tendencies. Delve into the mystical and magickal world of witchcraft to discover the power within yourself.

Home and Hearth
Create Magick at Home

Your home serves as your spiritual headquarters, temple, and sanctuary—a place for healing, regrouping, recharging, and practicing honor and respect.

Here's how to infuse everyday life with more magick at home!

IN YOUR HOME

Your home serves as a powerhouse for safety, comfort, rejuvenation, and as a nurturing sanctuary. It's where we store your most precious belongings, rest, recharge, eat, and sleep. Ideally, it's a safe haven where you can peacefully close your eyes without worry.

HEART AND HEARTH

Traditionally, the hearth was the focal point of the home, where fires were lit for cooking and heating. This concept is often paralleled with the modern kitchen, which is considered the heart or hearth of the home.

SPIRITUAL HEADQUARTERS

In Japanese culture, the practice of removing shoes at the doorway of homes is widespread. This tradition is rooted in showing respect for the home and its owners, as well as maintaining cleanliness. It symbolically signifies leaving worries and stress outside, inviting positive energy into the home. This practice extends to shrines, temples, and some places of business, serving as a conscious act of gratitude, respect, and acknowledgment.

KITCHEN MAGICK

Kitchen magick involves infusing cooking with intentional energy and spells, using magickal plants, spices, and herbs. Cast iron cookware, favored for its ability to hold and amplify energy, is commonly used, while stainless steel is recommended for liquid-based meals. By adding deliberate ingredients and stirring with intention, you will release spells and create delicious meals that nourish both body and spirit.

witchcraftspellsmagick.com

Everyday Magick

**Where the mundane transforms into the mystical,
and the ordinary becomes extraordinary.**

Morning Magick - Start your day with a touch of enchantment. As you stir your morning tea or coffee, repeat a spell, infusing each swirl with intentions for the day ahead.

Morning Affirmations - Start your day with empowering affirmations. Repeat them aloud or silently to affirm your worth, strength, and intentions. Let them uplift your spirit and align your energy with your goals.

Shower Ritual - Transform your shower into a renewal ritual. Let water wash away worries, concerns, and stress, revitalizing your energy.

Grounding Practice - Connect with the earth beneath your feet, grounding yourself in the present moment. Feel the solidity of the ground, honoring the natural world that surrounds you and fostering a deep sense of connection.

Home Protection - Walk around your home, drawing or visualizing a protective pentagram symbol with each step. Infuse your path with intention, visualizing a shield of positive energy surrounding yourself and your space.

Gratitude Fold - Turn the chore of folding laundry into a mindful practice of gratitude. As you fold each item, express gratitude for its purpose and the abundance it represents in your life.

Mindful Meals - Before eating, express gratitude for the nourishment and abundance provided by your meal. Cultivate mindfulness as you eat, savoring each bite and acknowledging the process of food from farm to table.

Cosmic Connection - Spend a few moments each night under the night sky, connecting with the cosmic energies above. Feel the vastness of the universe enveloping you, inspiring awe and wonder.

Crown
Third Eye
Throat
Heart
Solar Plexus
Sacral/Belly
Root/Base

Grounding and balancing meditation techniques can assist you in attaining a tranquil mind and a harmonized body. These practices have the potential to augment your intuitive abilities and facilitate deeper engagement with spell work, rituals, and other aspects of witchcraft. By directing your attention to your breath and establishing a connection with the earth, you can discover and ultimately attain inner peace and equilibrium.

Energy Work

GROUNDING AND BALANCING MEDITATION

Achieve a sense of balance and inner peace with grounding and balancing meditation techniques. By connecting with universal cosmic energy and grounding yourself, you will feel calm and clarity in your daily life.

1. Invite a calm and healing vibration of energy around you by raising your arms above your head, reaching towards the universe, and visualizing divine energies pouring into your crown.

2. Draw the energy downward through your crown to your third eye, visualizing it radiating outward. Allow the energy to return within you, then guide it further down to your throat.

3. Touch your throat center, the centre of self-expression and speech.

4. Continue to guide the energy through you, **reaching your heart.** Experience wholeness, self-love, and completeness.

5. Direct the energy down to your **solar plexus,** the centre of vitality, healing, and strength.

6. Touching your belly, the center of well-being, feel its nurturing energy. Connect to your root base, forming a downward triangle with your hands.

7. Lastly, push your hands downwards, **grounding the energy back to Earth.**

2025 Book of Shadows   49

Inner Witch

Step into the realm of the Inner Witch, where everyday moments are infused with magick and intention. Here, intuition reigns supreme as a guiding force, leading us on a path of self-discovery and empowerment.

"Never question your 'knowing'; it's intuition —a power portal of guidance."

- Consciously consume water.
- Get 8+ hours of sleep.
- Write in your Magickal Grimoire.
- Set up your monthly altar.
- Eat healthy and nutritious food.
- Meditate privately outdoors.
- Focus on an intention in the moonlight.
- Read a book about witchcraft.
- Walk barefoot on grass or sand.
- Listen to the sounds of nature.
- Take a shower and wash away your worries.
- Create a witch-inspired mood board.
- Spend time alone.
- Massage your face, neck, and body.
- Bake ritual cookies or cake.
- Set an intention for the month ahead.

Energy Balancing

Cultivate balance, centering, and alignment to unlock inner peace and clarity, essential for well-being and potent tools in spell work, ritual, and magick.

CHAKRA ENERGY CENTRES

Each chakra is a gateway to unique realms of consciousness and vitality, offering insights into holistic well-being.

ROOT/BASE
Grounding, self-worth, stability, security, the foundation of basic needs.

SACRAL/BELLY
Centre of wellbeing, sexual energy, pleasure, reproduction, and creativity.

SOLAR PLEXUS
Connect to your core energy source, your vitality, virility and spiritual power.

HEART
Absolute completeness, self-love, relationships, discipline and self-control.

THROAT
Communication, listening, speech, self-expression. Offers an opening to honest self.

THIRD EYE
The middle of your forehead, foresight, opens intuition and powers understanding.

CROWN
Mystic, powerful divine connection, at the top of your head. Access a higher state of consciousness.

witchcraftspellsmagick.com

Protection and Balance Meditation

Prepare for meditation by selecting a quiet, private space where you won't be disturbed. Seated or lying down, close your eyes and connect with the cosmic energy while grounding yourself.

1. Palms out and open, visualize holding calm, healing, protective energy vibrating in your hands.
2. Transform this energy into a sphere of protection, envisioning it expanding above and below you, encasing your body.
3. Maintain focus through your third eye. Repeat *'No thoughts shall enter my mind'* to prevent distractions.
4. Visualize a stream of positive healing energy from your third eye. Hold this state as long as possible.

After meditation, bring your hands together and push them down to he ground, elease excess energy, reconnecting with Earth's grounding energy.

WITCH TIP:
Always stay grounded after working with any type of energy—divine, metaphysical, elemental, animal, or otherwise. Remember to ground yourself before and after!

Grounding Ritual

This grounding ritual is for balance, clarity, and rejuvenation of your energy. It's the perfect start and finish for any spell work, ritual, or magickal practice.

Earthing Ritual Steps

1. **Cleanse yourself and your ritual space** using a smudge stick, palo santo, incense, or essential oils.
2. **Sit comfortably,** holding a grounding crystal or stone.
3. **Close your eyes and engage with your surroundings,** allowing yourself to be present with the ground/earth beneath you—completely comfortable in yourself.
4. **Imagine roots growing from the base of your body,** cascading downwards into the ground. Visualize these roots extending as deep and wide as you need.
5. **Ground your roots;** imagine your worries, concerns, stresses, and hassles leaving your body and entering the earth beneath. The earth's energy is powerful and will receive your mortal woes without prejudice or pushback.
6. **Focus on your breath;** breathe slowly in and out.
7. **When you are ready, intentionally open your eyes and express gratitude** to the earth for restoring your inner peace and balance.

Illustration based on classic Witchcraft altar setup.

Labels: Candles, Altar Cloth, Mother Nature, Deity Statue, Offering, Chalice, Incense, Crystals, Bell, Athamé, Pentacle, Offering, Salt, Wand

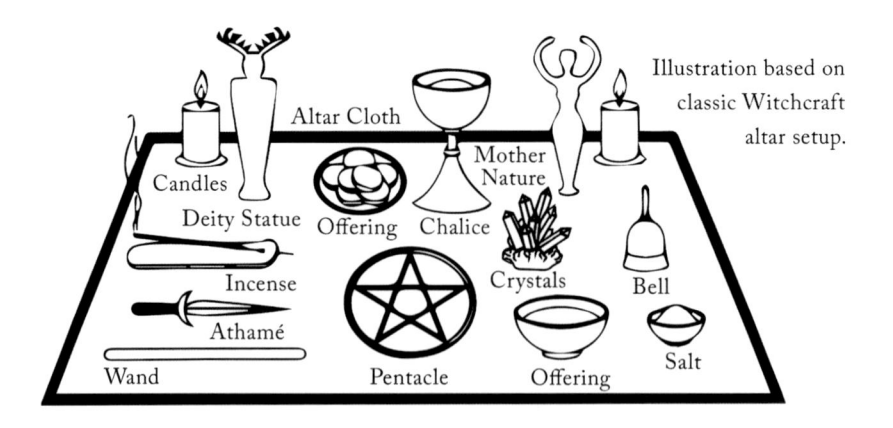

A Witch's Altar

**Altars are used across many spiritual paths
as dedicated places to honor and worship.**

A witch's altar is a personal or shared space to focus on specific energy
or energies with intention. An altar's intention may pay respect to divine
or elemental energies, past loved ones, seasonal celebrations,
or anything you choose of worth for deep reflection.

What to Include on an Altar

When crafting an altar, it's crucial to incorporate objects
that resonate with its intended purpose or represent the energies
you seek to invoke. Each item should be chosen thoughtfully
and placed with intention, as they carry deep symbolic meaning.

Depending on the altar's purpose, some items may be used regularly
while others are reserved for special occasions. It's customary to include
an offering as a gesture of respect and gratitude, which can range
from food and spices to candles or natural elements such as flowers,
foliage, seeds, sticks, leaves, and other symbolic natural items
that hold significance to your spiritual practice. These elements
help establish a sacred space and reinforce the altar's intended purpose.

witchcraftspellsmagick.com

Core Altar Checklist

A core setup list for creating a witch's altar. Include an object to represent each elemental energy on your altar: **Earth - Pentacle | Water - Chalice | Air - Incense or Diffuser | Fire - Candle**

Where should you set up a witch's altar? There are many choices for spaces you can use for your altar, whether temporary or permanent. This could be a stool, shelf, table, box or chest lid, or even a natural altar for outdoor practice.

- ☐ Altar cloth
- ☐ Pentacle (Earth)
- ☐ Incense / Diffuser (Air)
- ☐ Cup / Chalice (Water)
- ☐ Candles (Fire)
- ☐ Crystals
- ☐ Statues of Deities or Deity
- ☐ Offering / Blessing (Cake, biscuits, bread, a bowl of salt, spices, or herbs)
- ☐ Seasonal decorations (Flowers, herbs, fruit, vegetables)
- ☐ Objects and tools significant to the intention of the altar
- ☐ Bell (A bell chime shifts consciousness when engaging with your altar.)

Monthly Altars... Each month, there are plenty of ideas for what to include on your altar.

Notes: _____

_____
_____
_____
_____
_____
_____

Soulful Ambience

> **CENTRE AND ALIGN YOURSELF**
> Soulful ambience is all about being present in the moment and connecting with your body and spirit. Take a moment to relax and feel the ground beneath you, listen to the sounds, feel the breeze—be aware of your surroundings.

Thought Control

The practice of meditation involves achieving a state of focused relaxation and mental clarity. It requires deliberate and intentional effort to control one's thoughts and energy flow throughout the body. The practice of thought control is often used in meditation to help individuals focus and clear their minds.

One technique is to actively block any thoughts that may arise by telling oneself "no thoughts allowed." This can be a helpful tool for those who struggle with distracting or intrusive thoughts during meditation.

However, it is important to remember that thoughts are a natural part of the human experience, and it is okay to acknowledge and observe them without judgment.

Meditation does require a quiet space where you can allow yourself to be. The practice of thought control involves various techniques, another of which is to focus on a simple shape or form. Shapes like circles, squares, or stars are particularly effective. By repeatedly visualizing a shape and transforming it into a 3-dimensional form, you can enter into a deeper visionary experience. This technique will help you gain greater control over your thoughts and emotions.

Align your Mood

Aromatics serve as meditation and medicinal triggers. Try essential oils such as frankincense, ylang-ylang, cedarwood, or lavender (choose organic whenever possible).

You might like to use smudging, a sacred practice of the Indigenous peoples of the Americas involving burning sage to clear negative energies from people, objects, and environments.

For maximum comfort, grab a cushion and settle into a comfortable seating position. Experiment with sound by trying music, chanting, or humming. Sometimes, the absence of sound, in the form of silence, is the best choice.

witchcraftspellsmagick.com

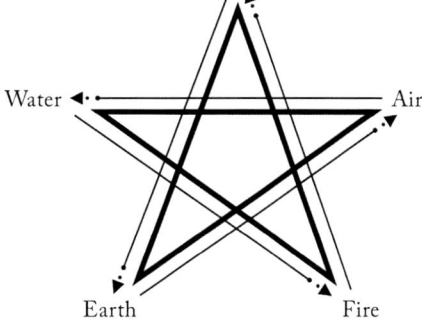

Mindful Magick
Why Meditate?

Meditation has numerous benefits, including the ability to cultivate and nurture inner peace and calmness even amidst chaos. It can also help you align your energy with the universe and improve your overall well-being. When practicing witchcraft, mastering a harmonious and calm state of mind through meditation can be especially beneficial in enhancing your craft.
So, why meditate? To improve your mental and spiritual health.

INVOKING
Clockwise or sun-wise motion
Calling forth, summoning, or requesting
Use: Invoke deities, the elements, or spirits to collaborate with you.

BANISHING
Counterclockwise or moon-wise motion
Removing negative energies
Use: Ritual purification, protection, and preparing magickal space for practice.

PROTECTIVE SYMBOLISM
To add extra protection to your day, try this technique.
Throughout the day, whether during spell work or just going about your business, visualize a five-pointed pentagram star in your mind. Hold onto this image and project it outwards in front of you. Keep drawing the star repeatedly, creating a protective force field around you. Use this technique as often as you need for added magickal support.

Banishing (Counterclockwise): Moon wise.

Circle Casting Directions

Invoking (Clockwise): Sun wise.

Sacred Space
What is a Sacred Circle?

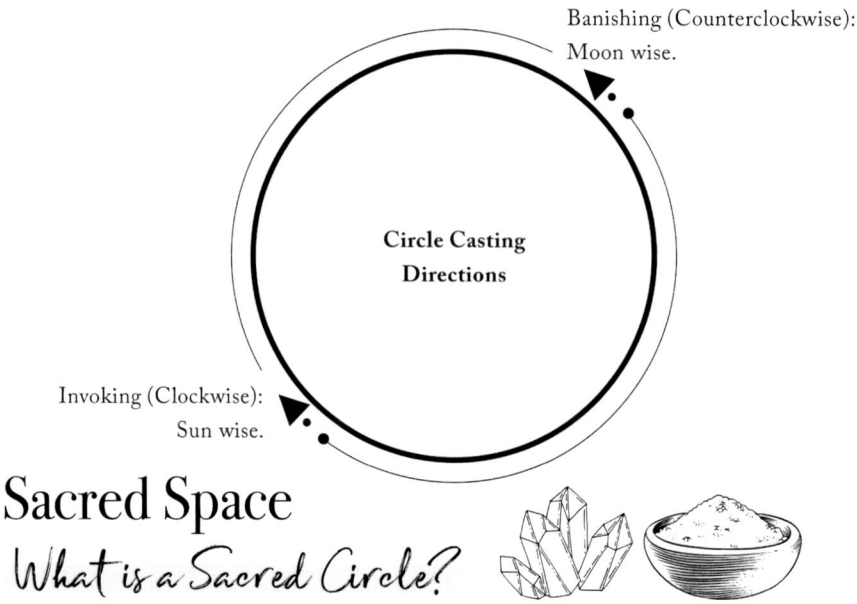

Witches cast circles for many reasons: protection during spell work, meditation, manifestation, divination, and throughout the day when needed. This can involve literal or psychic circle casting, both aimed at surrounding you with protective energy.

Physical Circle Casting

There are many creative ways to cast a physical circle. You might use a circular rug or sprinkle salt in a circle on your floor. Include crystals, candles, tape, chalk, or mark outdoors in dirt, sand, flour, or salt.

Walk the circumference of your circle with focus and intent, using tools like an athamé, wand, smudge stick, palo santo, candle, or incense. You might also create a protective pentagram with masking tape, salt, or psychically.

The five-pointed pentagram star symbolizes Earth, Water, Air, Fire, with the fifth point representing Spirit, the eternal universe, and the divine in the metaphysical, spiritual, and cosmic realms. When encompassed in a circle, it is completed, with neither beginning nor end, representing eternal energy and power.

Psychic Circle Casting

Visualize a sphere of white energy forming in your hands. Expand this sphere until it surrounds you completely, with you at the center. This technique establishes a sacred space for psychic work and shields you from negative energies.

witchcraftspellsmagick.com

Manifesting

Spells are the manifestation of will!
Also known as incantations, enchantments, or bewitchery,
spells trigger a magickal response that transforms energy and alters outcomes.

Spells can be spoken, written, thought, chanted, or sung.
Achieving a successful spell requires an alchemical mix of components.
Witches use spells to manifest their desired outcomes formed from intentions.

Manifesting spells is ideally done during a ritual.
Ritual is the ceremonial practice of magick.

While manifesting through visualization is possible, it's considered extremely advanced witchcraft. For the most part, it's best to support manifesting by ensuring you have any corresponding magickal tools and necessary items before you start.

Ultimately, you want your spells to work—practice and patience!
Why do some spells not work?
As a witch, you feel a certain obligation to cast spells that work.
Fundamentally, spells might not work for many reasons:
1. Be patient—spells don't often work instantly.
2. Are you feeling it? Do you believe in the work you are doing?
3. Check correspondences—the moon, time of day, season, direction, and surrounding energies.
4. Have you repeated the spell? If you don't succeed, try again.

Why do spells work?
Spells require a certain alchemical mix of elements, components, energy, and intention, all in the correct space and time. As you gain more experience, you will become more capable of casting spells that work.
You are a channel for the magickal energy; do not rely solely on your own.

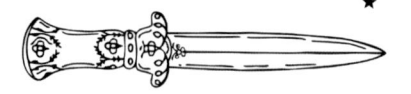

Magickal Intent

Intention

An intention is a purpose or reason for why you are creating a spell or performing a ritual. This may be for love, good fortune, or to banish something from your life. Ethics vary on whether spells should be used on other people. At first, try only spells connected to yourself. Spells can rapidly get out of control and are hard to stop once in motion.

Center and Align

Center your core by aligning your chakra energy centers as you meditate. Visualize roots attached to your feet; allow them to explore and secure themselves into the earth beneath your feet. Connect and open your mind —align your crown chakra with the divine energies above.

Breathe deeply, continuing with conscious, deep, and long breaths. Balance your energy; on the left side of your body, feel the water energies around and within you. On the right side, feel the fire energies of warmth, passion, and strength.

Open Heart

Surrender and relax your body into a calm, comfortable, and peaceful state. Invoke energy from the four elements: **Earth, Air, Fire, and Water; not your core energy!**

Space

You have superpower intuition! Use your intuition to feel the energy of your space you are working in; if it's flat, so will be your working.

Correspondening Energies

Time of day, phase of the moon, season, weather, planetary alignment, colors, herbs, symbols, crystals, and divination tools.

witchcraftspellsmagick.com

Planning Intentions

In order to manifest your intentions successfully, it's important to plan them out carefully. This layout can help you organize your thoughts and gather the necessary information to make your intentions a reality. As you become more knowledgeable about the process of manifestation, you'll become more skilled at shaping your desired outcome through intentional magick. Manifesting is all about turning your thoughts into reality, take the time to plan your intentions carefully and let the magick happen.

Sketch your intention

Intention: _____ **Date:** _____

Description / Characteristics: _____

_____

_____

Desired outcome: _____

Energies (moon phase, planetary alignment, season, time of day): _____

_____

Correspondences (colours, flowers, crystals, herbs): _____

_____

Observations: _____

Witchcraft Ritual
Circle Casting Steps

1. PREPARATION
Gather objects and prepare the ritual space with candles, crystals, and a circle of white energy.

2. PURIFICATION
Cleanse yourself and the space, whether by showering, bathing, or choosing ritual attire and jewelry.

3. CASTING
Walk the circle's circumference, creating either a Physical or Psychic circle using tools like an athamé, wand, or smudge stick.

4. INVOCATION
Introduce the energies you'll work with, invoking the elements, deities, spirit guides, or other energies.

5. INTENTION
Use a tool or finger to draw a pentagram, stating your intention clearly.

6. RITUAL PRACTICE
Engage in meditation, divination, chanting, spell work, or other magickal practices that align with your intention.

7. CLOSING
Conclude the ritual by dancing, focusing on a lit candle, or sipping from the chalice.

8. GRATITUDE AND REFLECTION
Thank the elements, deities, and fellow witches involved, sharing food and reflecting on the experience. Record your insights.

witchcraftspellsmagick.com

Sketch your intention

Planning Rituals

Whether for a small, personal gathering or an elaborate ceremony, planning and preparation enrich your practice. Rituals occur during full moons, Witches' Sabbats, or whenever you seek divine or cosmic protection. No matter quick or extensive, keeping track of tasks is crucial. The level of planning needed varies with your familiarity with the ritual. By dedicating time to plan and prepare, you ensure a more successful and meaningful practice and outcome.

Ritual: _____ **Date:** _____

Description / Characteristics: _____

_____

_____

Desired outcome: _____

Energies (moon phase, planetary alignment, season, time of day): _____

_____

Correspondences (colours, flowers, crystals, herbs): _____

_____

Observations: _____

PART 4

Diary

Document your Witchcraft Journey through the Calendar Year
The Practicing Witch Diary - Book of Shadows 2025

Explore a wealth of practicing ideas, altar setups, spells, rituals, intention setting, correspondences, and lunar cycles month by month.

This diary serves as a record of your magickal journey, supporting your personal, spiritual, and soulful growth throughout the year.

Whether you prefer reading, writing, drawing, or scrapbooking, it offers ample space to document your witchcraft practices, experiences, spells, meditations, lunar cycles, dreams, tarot readings, and more.

As a practicing witch, you understand the importance of conscious and intentional witchcraft practices for the benefits of spiritual growth.

This diary will deepen your connection to the mystical, guiding you to manifest magick and access your inner power.

Through your written word, drawn forms, shapes, sigils, and images, you manifest change and gain insights to reflect on your progress.

Remain mindful, humble, and grateful, respecting the energies around you.

As you journey along your magickal path, remember that the energy you emit will shape the energy you attract.

witchcraftspellsmagick.com

2025

January

M	T	W	T	F	S	S
		1	2	3	4	5
6	7	8	9	10	11	12
13	14	15	16	17	18	19
20	21	22	23	24	25	26
27	28	29	30	31		

February

M	T	W	T	F	S	S
					1	2
3	4	5	6	7	8	9
10	11	12	13	14	15	16
17	18	19	20	21	22	23
24	25	26	27	28		

March

M	T	W	T	F	S	S
					1	2
3	4	5	6	7	8	9
10	11	12	13	14	15	16
17	18	19	20	21	22	23
24	25	26	27	28	29	30
31						

April

M	T	W	T	F	S	S
	1	2	3	4	5	6
7	8	9	10	11	12	13
14	15	16	17	18	19	20
21	22	23	24	25	26	27
28	29	30				

May

M	T	W	T	F	S	S
			1	2	3	4
5	6	7	8	9	10	11
12	13	14	15	16	17	18
19	20	21	22	23	24	25
26	27	28	29	30	31	

June

M	T	W	T	F	S	S
						1
2	3	4	5	6	7	8
9	10	11	12	13	14	15
16	17	18	19	20	21	22
23	24	25	26	27	28	29
30						

July

M	T	W	T	F	S	S
	1	2	3	4	5	6
7	8	9	10	11	12	13
14	15	16	17	18	19	20
21	22	23	24	25	26	27
28	29	30	31			

August

M	T	W	T	F	S	S
				1	2	3
4	5	6	7	8	9	10
11	12	13	14	15	16	17
18	19	20	21	22	23	24
25	26	27	28	29	30	31

September

M	T	W	T	F	S	S
1	2	3	4	5	6	7
8	9	10	11	12	13	14
15	16	17	18	19	20	21
22	23	24	25	26	27	28
29	30					

October

M	T	W	T	F	S	S
		1	2	3	4	5
6	7	8	9	10	11	12
13	14	15	16	17	18	19
20	21	22	23	24	25	26
27	28	29	30	31		

November

M	T	W	T	F	S	S
					1	2
3	4	5	6	7	8	9
10	11	12	13	14	15	16
17	18	19	20	21	22	23
24	25	26	27	28	29	30

December

M	T	W	T	F	S	S
1	2	3	4	5	6	7
8	9	10	11	12	13	14
15	16	17	18	19	20	21
22	23	24	25	26	27	28
29	30	31				

January 2025

Monday	Tuesday	Wednesday	Thursday	Friday
30	31	1	2	3
6 *First Quarter Moon*	7	8	9	10
13 *Full Moon in Cancer*	14	15	16	17
20	21 *Last Quarter Moon*	22	23	24
27	28	29 *Dark Moon*	30	31
3	4	5	6	7

witchcraftspellsmagick.com

Saturday	Sunday
4	5
11	12
18	19
25	26
1	2
8	9

This Month

Lunar Cycle Intention:

_____

_____

Most Important Events:

1. _____
2. _____
3. _____
4. _____
5. _____

To Do List:

○ _____
○ _____
○ _____
○ _____
○ _____
○ _____
○ _____

Notes & Thoughts:

January 2025

NEW BEGINNINGS

January marks the dawn of new beginnings, a time to shed the weight of the past and embrace the promise of fresh starts.

While Samhain signals the Pagan New Year with its theme of rebirth, January signifies the start of the calendar year, ushering in opportunities for renewal and growth. For modern witches, January symbolizes a clean slate—a chance to purify altar spaces, cleanse tools, and prepare for the magickal journey ahead. It's a time to set intentions and lay the groundwork for manifestations in the months to come.

Named after the Roman god Janus, January derives its significance from the Latin word 'ianua', meaning a double-doored entrance. This symbolism speaks to the duality of beginnings and passages, inviting us to step boldly through the threshold of possibility into a new year of spiritual exploration and discovery.

This Month's
RITUAL INSPIRATION

MANIFESTATION BOX - The Power of Intention

Craft a manifestation box, a sacred vessel for manifesting your desires in the coming year. Draw or write your intentions on pieces of paper and place them inside the box, infusing them with your will and purpose. During a ritual, bless the box and consecrate it on your altar, imbuing it with energy to fuel your manifestations throughout the year. Safely tuck it away for the year once you've changed your altar, remembering to manifest intentionally, through your will. The box becomes a vessel of energy with a purpose.

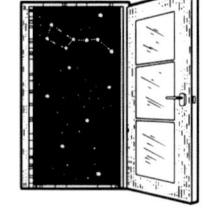

DOORWAY BLESSING - Magickal Purification

A doorway cleansing and blessing will invite positive energy into your home and ward off negativity. Sprinkle or place small bowls of salt around your doorways, or hang a small bag filled with salt at the threshold. As you do so, visualize a protective barrier forming, shielding your home from unwanted influences and creating a sanctuary of peace and positivity.

witchcraftspellsmagick.com

Tarot Reading

Monthly Tarot readings offer you valuable guidance and insight for the month ahead. To start, shuffle your cards for at least 30-40 seconds while focusing on a specific question or area of your life that you would like guidance on.

When you're ready, lay down the top three cards to represent the past, present, and future. For further details on tarot, visit witchcraftspellsmagick.com

Past
Where you have been.

Current
Where you are now.

Future
Where you are going next.

Deck: _____ **Date:** _____

Card 1 - Past: _____
_____
_____

Card 2 - Current: _____
_____
_____

Card 3 - Future: _____
_____
_____

January Magickal Correspondences

January, the start of the calendar year, invites fresh starts. While Samhain marks the Pagan New Year, January offers a unique opportunity for renewal and growth.

This month symbolizes a clean slate—a chance to purify altar spaces, cleanse tools, and prepare for the magickal journey ahead. Embrace the promise of spiritual exploration, setting intentions for the year ahead.

Animals: Dragon, Fox, Pheasant, Rabbit, Snake, Wolf
Colours: Black, Blue, Gold, White, Yellow
Crystals: Amber, Clear quartz, Garnet, Jet, Onyx, Moonstone, Aquamarine
Flowers: Camellia, Carnation, Galanthus, Lily, Rose, Thistle
Fruits: Apple, Lemon, Orange, Pomegranate, Grapefruit
Herbs: Cypress, Marjoram, Sage, Basil, Mint
Aromatics: Dragon's blood, Frankincense, Sage, Sandalwood, Myrrh, Patchouli
Spices: Cinnamon, Clove, Nutmeg, Cardamom
Trees: Birch, Oak, Spruce, Willow, Cedar

ALTAR CHECKLIST
New Beginnings, Renewal & Growth
Altar Setup Basics - Start with the Elements:
Earth: Pentacle | Water: Chalice
Air: Incense or Diffuser | Fire: Candle

Additional Ideas:
- Statues or symbols of renewal
- Cauldron
- Crystals
- Witch jars
- Manifestation box
- Altar besom
- Bell (a chime shifts consciousness)
- Crystal ball
- Tarot

Notes & Thoughts:

witchcraftspellsmagick.com

Sketch Your Altar Setup

Altar Planning

Creating a monthly altar helps you align with the cycles of nature and set focused intentions for your magickal practices.

Use this template to plan and organize your altar setup, ensuring that each element supports your intention and enhances your connection to the energies of the month. Thoughtful planning and intentional arrangement of your altar will amplify your magick and help manifest your desired outcomes.

Intention: _____

Desired Outcome: _____

Notable Monthly Energies: _____

_____

Altar Aesthetics: _____

_____

_____

Altar Elements: _____

_____

Intentions

Utilize an intention to form the foundation of your manifestation, which means creating the desired outcome in accordance with your will. Intentions are the purpose or reason for why you are creating a spell or engaging in any magickal practice.

This may be for love, good fortune, or to banish something from your life. When starting spell work, focus on intentions connected to yourself only, not others.

Even good magick can take on a life of its own and be unexpected, often tripling in power and energy and coming back to you —good, bad, or in a twisted form. When the time is right, choose as many intentions and cast as many protection charms, wellness, success, good fortune, and hope for love or companionship as you can manifest each month.

Intentions are woven into spells—spells hold the energy and the intention, working by following the path of least resistance. Start slow and small rather than aiming for unstoppable tidal waves.

Intention Setting

This month, choose 1-4 intentions to focus on, whether for the entire month, lunar cycle, or one per week, depending on how much you practice.

    Setting clear and focused intentions is crucial in your magickal practice. Narrowing your focus helps channel your energy more effectively. Whether for self-improvement, attracting positivity, or banishing negativity, these intentions guide your magickal work and keep you aligned with your goals.

    Review and select your intentions this month. Consistency and clarity are key, allowing your intentions to manifest through dedicated practice, repetition, effort, and willpower.

Adventure	Authenticity	Balance
Calm	Career	Change
Comfort	Communication	Community
Culture	Divine wisdom	Education
Energy	Family	Freedom
Friends	Fun	Growth
Happiness	Health	Honesty
Honoring	Integrity	Knowledge
Peace	Relationships	Resilience
Respect	Security	Self
Success	Travel	Trust
Wealth	Will	Wisdom

Spell Casting
TRANSFORM AN INTENTION INTO A SPELL

Crafting a spell involves careful planning and aligning various elements that resonate with your desired outcome.

Utilize spells to transform your intentions into reality. Use this template to plan and organize your spell work. Ensure each component supports and aligns with your intention, enhancing your magick with energy. By thoughtfully and mindfully selecting and arranging spell elements, you can amplify your magick and increase the effectiveness of your spell work. With focused intent and deliberate action, you will manifest your desires and achieve your goals.

Making Magick

When casting spells, consider which energies support your intention. Determine which correspondences, moon phases, planetary alignments, seasons, or times of day are best. Carefully selecting these elements enhances your spell's power and effectiveness.

Repetition Magick

Repetition Magick involves repeating your entire spell multiple times to strengthen the likelihood of achieving your desired outcome. This intensifies the energy and makes your spell more effective.

Never spell and tell before a spell has worked! It can muddle and redirect your focused energy, leading to negative results.

Spell 1

Intention: _____

_____

Desired Outcome: _____

_____

_____

_____

Correspondences: _____

_____

_____

_____

_____

_____

_____

_____

Spell 2

Intention: _____

_____

Desired Outcome: _____

_____

_____

_____

Correspondences: _____

_____

_____

_____

_____

_____

_____

Spell 3

Intention: _____

_____

Desired Outcome: _____

_____

_____

_____

Correspondences: _____

_____

_____

_____

_____

_____

_____

Spells are the manifestation of your will!

Spells are a powerful tool for you to work with to manifest your desires. By setting a clear intention and casting a spell during a ritual, you can transform energy and bend outcomes to your will. These incantations, also known as enchantments or bewitchery, take many forms—spoken, written, thought, chanted, or sung. Successful spell work requires an alchemical mix of components and a lot of practice and patience. With dedication and focus, you can utilize the power of spells to create your desired outcome.

Ritual Preparation

SACRED SPACE AND CIRCLE CASTING STEPS

Cast a circle before spell and ritual work, or anytime you want to invoke protection and create a sacred space. Here are some steps to guide you:

1. Preparation
Collect objects and prepare your space for ritual or spell work.

2. Purification
Cleanse the space and yourself.

3. Casting
Create a physical or psychic circle for protection and manifestation.

4. Invocation
Introduce the energies you intend to work with. Invocation: *"I/we graciously invoke you..."*

5. Intention
Use your tool to draw a pentagram and state your intention.

6. Ritual Practice
Meditation, trance work, psychic divination, dance, chanting, spell work...

7. Closing
Dance, sing, or share offerings.

8. Gratitude and Reflection
Give thanks to the divine, metaphysical, elemental, spirit, and mortal energies you have worked with.

Ritual 1

Intention: _____

Desired Outcome: _____

Notable Monthly Energies: _____

_____

Altar Aesthetics: _____

_____

Altar Elements: _____

_____

_____

witchcraftspellsmagick.com

Ritual 2

Intention: _____

Desired Outcome: _____

Notable Monthly Energies: _____

_____

Altar Aesthetics: _____

_____

Altar Elements: _____

_____

_____

> 1. Preparation, 2. Purification, 3. Casting, 4. Invocation,
> 5. Intention, 6. Ritual Practice, 7. Closing, 8. Gratitude and Reflection

Ritual 3

Intention: _____

Desired Outcome: _____

Notable Monthly Energies: _____

_____

Altar Aesthetics: _____

_____

Altar Elements: _____

_____

_____

January 2025

NOTES	To do

1st WEDNESDAY	2nd THURSDAY

Magickal Focus:_____

Daily Affirmation: _____

_____

Reflective Journal Keywords: _____

Magickal Focus:_____

Daily Affirmation: _____

_____

Reflective Journal Keywords: _____

witchcraftspellsmagick.com

3rd FRIDAY

Magickal Focus: _____

Daily Affirmation: _____

_____

Reflective Journal Keywords: _____

_____

4th SATURDAY

Magickal Focus: _____

Daily Affirmation: _____

_____

Reflective Journal Keywords: _____

_____

5th SUNDAY

Magickal Focus: _____

Daily Affirmation: _____

_____

Reflective Journal Keywords: _____

_____

To do

January 2025

6th MONDAY

First Quarter Moon

Magickal Focus: _____

Daily Affirmation: _____

_____

Reflective Journal Keywords: _____

_____

7th TUESDAY

Magickal Focus: _____

Daily Affirmation: _____

_____

Reflective Journal Keywords: _____

_____

8th WEDNESDAY

Magickal Focus: _____

Daily Affirmation: _____

_____

Reflective Journal Keywords: _____

_____

9th THURSDAY

Magickal Focus: _____

Daily Affirmation: _____

_____

Reflective Journal Keywords: _____

_____

10th FRIDAY	**11th SATURDAY**
Magickal Focus:_____ Daily Affirmation:_____ _____ Reflective Journal Keywords:_____ _____	Magickal Focus:_____ Daily Affirmation:_____ _____ Reflective Journal Keywords:_____ _____
12th SUNDAY	**To do**
Magickal Focus:_____ Daily Affirmation:_____ _____ Reflective Journal Keywords:_____ _____	

January 2025

13th MONDAY	14th TUESDAY
Full Moon Magickal Focus: _____ Daily Affirmation: _____ _____ Reflective Journal Keywords: _____ _____	 Magickal Focus: _____ Daily Affirmation: _____ _____ Reflective Journal Keywords: _____ _____
15th WEDNESDAY	**16th THURSDAY**
      Magickal Focus: _____ Daily Affirmation: _____ _____ Reflective Journal Keywords: _____ _____	 Magickal Focus: _____ Daily Affirmation: _____ _____ Reflective Journal Keywords: _____ _____

witchcraftspellsmagick.com

17th FRIDAY

Magickal Focus: _____

Daily Affirmation: _____
_____

Reflective Journal Keywords: _____
_____

18th SATURDAY

Magickal Focus: _____

Daily Affirmation: _____
_____

Reflective Journal Keywords: _____
_____

19th SUNDAY

Magickal Focus: _____

Daily Affirmation: _____
_____

Reflective Journal Keywords: _____
_____

To do

January 2025

20th MONDAY	21st TUESDAY
	Last Quarter Moon
Magickal Focus: _____	Magickal Focus: _____
Daily Affirmation: _____	Daily Affirmation: _____
Reflective Journal Keywords: _____	Reflective Journal Keywords: _____

22nd WEDNESDAY	23rd THURSDAY
Magickal Focus: _____	Magickal Focus: _____
Daily Affirmation: _____	Daily Affirmation: _____
Reflective Journal Keywords: _____	Reflective Journal Keywords: _____

witchcraftspellsmagick.com

24th FRIDAY	25th SATURDAY
Magickal Focus:_____ Daily Affirmation:_____ _____ Reflective Journal Keywords:_____ _____	Magickal Focus:_____ Daily Affirmation:_____ _____ Reflective Journal Keywords:_____ _____
26th SUNDAY	**To do**
Magickal Focus:_____ Daily Affirmation:_____ _____ Reflective Journal Keywords:_____ _____	

January 2025

27th MONDAY

Magickal Focus: _____

Daily Affirmation: _____
_____

Reflective Journal Keywords: _____
_____

28th TUESDAY

Magickal Focus: _____

Daily Affirmation: _____
_____

Reflective Journal Keywords: _____
_____

29th WEDNESDAY

●
Dark Moon

Magickal Focus: _____

Daily Affirmation: _____
_____

Reflective Journal Keywords: _____
_____

30th THURSDAY

Magickal Focus: _____

Daily Affirmation: _____
_____

Reflective Journal Keywords: _____
_____

31st FRIDAY

Magickal Focus: _____

Daily Affirmation: _____

_____

Reflective Journal Keywords: _____

_____

NOTES

NOTES

To do

February 2025

Monday	Tuesday	Wednesday	Thursday	Friday
27	28	29	30	31
3	4	5 *First Quarter Moon*	6	7
10	11	12 *Full Moon in Leo*	13	14
17	18	19	20 *Last Quarter Moon*	21
24	25	26 *Dark Moon*	27	28
3	4	5	6	7

witchcraftspellsmagick.com

Saturday	Sunday
1 *Imbolc*	2
8	9
15	16
22	23
1	2
8	9

This Month

Lunar Cycle Intention:

_____

_____

Most Important Events:

1. _____
2. _____
3. _____
4. _____
5. _____

To Do List:

○ _____
○ _____
○ _____
○ _____
○ _____
○ _____
○ _____

Notes & Thoughts:

February 2025

IMBOLC - Greater Witches' Sabbat

Imbolc is observed on the 1st of February in the Northern Hemisphere and the 1st of August in the Southern Hemisphere, is a sacred celebration steeped in ancient lore and rich symbolism.

This festival, also known as Oimelc, marks the awakening of spring and pays homage to the Goddess Brigid, revered for her association with fire, healing, and fertility.

As nature undergoes a profound transformation, Imbolc heralds a time of transition and renewal, where the dormant seeds of new life begin to stir beneath the Earth's surface. According to legend, Brigid traverses the land, bestowing warmth and fertility upon homes and fields alike, symbolizing the triumph of light over darkness. As we gather to honor the Horned God for his enduring strength and provision throughout the colder months, we do so with hearts aglow with candlelight and spirits brimming with hope, embracing the perpetual cycle of life's rhythms and the promise of rejuvenation that Imbolc brings.

This Month's
RITUAL INSPIRATION

BRIGID'S CROSS - Irish Goddess of Home and Hearth

Craft Brigid's Cross is a sacred symbol of protection and blessings, made using reeds or grasses. In ancient pagan lore, this cross was woven to ward off negativity and toxins, and to protect the home from disease and negativity. Forming a sun wheel a symbol and powerful amulet to add to your Imbolc altar and ritual practice.

IMBOLC CANDLES - Handmade Magick Candles

Infused with intention and crafted with care, homemade Imbolc candles will carry the energies of the season through your magickal practice. Enhance their potency by incorporating corresponding Imbolc essential oils, flowers, and herbs. Light the candles and indulge yourself in a ritual shower or bath, allowing the cleansing waters to wash away negative energy and revitalize your spirit, preparing you for the transformative energies of Imbolc.

witchcraftspellsmagick.com

Tarot Reading

Monthly Tarot readings offer you valuable guidance and insight for the month ahead. To start, shuffle your cards for at least 30-40 seconds while focusing on a specific question or area of your life that you would like guidance on.

When you're ready, lay down the top three cards to represent the past, present, and future. For further details on tarot, visit witchcraftspellsmagick.com

Past
Where you have been.

Current
Where you are now.

Future
Where you are going next.

Deck: _____ **Date:** _____

Card 1 - Past: _____
_____
_____

Card 2 - Current: _____
_____
_____

Card 3 - Future: _____
_____
_____

February Magickal Correspondences

February is a month of transition, as winter begins to give way to the early signs of spring. It's a time for purification, renewal, and preparing for the growth ahead.

The energies of February encourage introspection, setting intentions, and planting the seeds for future endeavors. The following correspondences are aligned with the magickal energies of February and can be used in your rituals and practices.

Animals - Dragon, Fox, Owl, Snake, Wolf
Aromatics - Cedarwood, Chamomile, Dragon's Blood, Frankincense, Myrrh, Sage
Colors - Gold, Green, Grey, Purple, Silver, White
Crystals - Amethyst, Bloodstone, Garnet, Malachite, Moonstone, Onyx, Turquoise
Flowers - Crocus, Daffodil, Daisy, Isis, Jasmine, Lavender, Snowdrop, Violet
Fruits - Apple, Cherry, Grape, Lemon, Orange, Strawberry
Herbs - Angelica, Basil, Bay Laurel, Mint, Rosemary, Thyme
Spices - Cinnamon, Clove, Red Pepper
Trees - Ash, Birch, Blackthorn, Rowan, Sycamore, Willow

ALTAR CHECKLIST
Fortune + Energy
Altar Setup Basics - Start with the Elements:
Earth: Pentacle | Water: Chalice
Air: Incense or Diffuser | Fire: Candle

Additional Ideas:
- Brigid's Cross
- Gratitude list
- Antlers
- White cloth
- Red cord
- Altar besom
- Bowl of nuts or seeds
- Greenery/Small plant
- Cinnamon & Spiced Apple Cake

Notes & Thoughts:

---

witchcraftspellsmagick.com

Sketch Your Altar Setup

Altar Planning

Creating a monthly altar helps you align with the cycles of nature and set focused intentions for your magickal practices.

Use this template to plan and organize your altar setup, ensuring that each element supports your intention and enhances your connection to the energies of the month. Thoughtful planning and intentional arrangement of your altar will amplify your magick and help manifest your desired outcomes.

Intention: _____

Desired Outcome: _____

Notable Monthly Energies: _____

_____

Altar Aesthetics: _____

_____

_____

Altar Elements: _____

_____

Intentions

Utilize an intention to form the foundation of your manifestation, which means creating the desired outcome in accordance with your will. Intentions are the purpose or reason for why you are creating a spell or engaging in any magickal practice.

This may be for love, good fortune, or to banish something from your life. When starting spell work, focus on intentions connected to yourself only, not others.

Even good magick can take on a life of its own and be unexpected, often tripling in power and energy and coming back to you —good, bad, or in a twisted form. When the time is right, choose as many intentions and cast as many protection charms, wellness, success, good fortune, and hope for love or companionship as you can manifest each month.

Intentions are woven into spells—spells hold the energy and the intention, working by following the path of least resistance. Start slow and small rather than aiming for unstoppable tidal waves.

Intention Setting

This month, choose 1-4 intentions to focus on, whether for the entire month, lunar cycle, or one per week, depending on how much you practice.

Setting clear and focused intentions is crucial in your magickal practice. Narrowing your focus helps channel your energy more effectively. Whether for self-improvement, attracting positivity, or banishing negativity, these intentions guide your magickal work and keep you aligned with your goals.

Review and select your intentions this month. Consistency and clarity are key, allowing your intentions to manifest through dedicated practice, repetition, effort, and willpower.

Adventure	Authenticity	Balance
Calm	Career	Change
Comfort	Communication	Community
Culture	Divine wisdom	Education
Energy	Family	Freedom
Friends	Fun	Growth
Happiness	Health	Honesty
Honoring	Integrity	Knowledge
Peace	Relationships	Resilience
Respect	Security	Self
Success	Travel	Trust
Wealth	Will	Wisdom

Spell Casting
TRANSFORM AN INTENTION INTO A SPELL

Crafting a spell involves careful planning and aligning various elements that resonate with your desired outcome.

Utilize spells to transform your intentions into reality. Use this template to plan and organize your spell work. Ensure each component supports and aligns with your intention, enhancing your magick with energy. By thoughtfully and mindfully selecting and arranging spell elements, you can amplify your magick and increase the effectiveness of your spell work. With focused intent and deliberate action, you will manifest your desires and achieve your goals.

Making Magick
When casting spells, consider which energies support your intention. Determine which correspondences, moon phases, planetary alignments, seasons, or times of day are best. Carefully selecting these elements enhances your spell's power and effectiveness.

Repetition Magick
Repetition Magick involves repeating your entire spell multiple times to strengthen the likelihood of achieving your desired outcome. This intensifies the energy and makes your spell more effective.

Never spell and tell before a spell has worked! It can muddle and redirect your focused energy, leading to negative results.

Spell 1

Intention: _____

_____

Desired Outcome: _____

_____

_____

_____

Correspondences: _____

_____

_____

_____

_____

_____

_____

_____

witchcraftspellsmagick.com

Spell 2

Intention: _____

_____

Desired Outcome: _____

_____

_____

_____

Correspondences: _____

_____

_____

_____

_____

_____

_____

Spell 3

Intention: _____

_____

Desired Outcome: _____

_____

_____

_____

Correspondences: _____

_____

_____

_____

_____

_____

_____

Spells are the manifestation of your will!

Spells are a powerful tool for you to work with to manifest your desires. By setting a clear intention and casting a spell during a ritual, you can transform energy and bend outcomes to your will. These incantations, also known as enchantments or bewitchery, take many forms—spoken, written, thought, chanted, or sung. Successful spell work requires an alchemical mix of components and a lot of practice and patience. With dedication and focus, you can utilize the power of spells to create your desired outcome.

Ritual Preparation

SACRED SPACE AND CIRCLE CASTING STEPS

Cast a circle before spell and ritual work, or anytime you want to invoke protection and create a sacred space. Here are some steps to guide you:

1. Preparation
Collect objects and prepare your space for ritual or spell work.

2. Purification
Cleanse the space and yourself.

3. Casting
Create a physical or psychic circle for protection and manifestation.

4. Invocation
Introduce the energies you intend to work with. Invocation: *"I/we graciously invoke you..."*

5. Intention
Use your tool to draw a pentagram and state your intention.

6. Ritual Practice
Meditation, trance work, psychic divination, dance, chanting, spell work...

7. Closing
Dance, sing, or share offerings.

8. Gratitude and Reflection
Give thanks to the divine, metaphysical, elemental, spirit, and mortal energies you have worked with.

Ritual 1

Intention: _____

Desired Outcome: _____

Notable Monthly Energies: _____

_____

Altar Aesthetics: _____

_____

Altar Elements: _____

_____

_____

Ritual 2

Intention: _____

Desired Outcome: _____

Notable Monthly Energies: _____

_____

Altar Aesthetics: _____

_____

Altar Elements: _____

_____

_____

1. Preparation, 2. Purification, 3. Casting, 4. Invocation,
5. Intention, 6. Ritual Practice, 7. Closing, 8. Gratitude and Reflection

Ritual 3

Intention: _____

Desired Outcome: _____

Notable Monthly Energies: _____

_____

Altar Aesthetics: _____

_____

Altar Elements: _____

_____

_____

February 2025

To do

NOTES

NOTES

To do

NOTES	**1st SATURDAY**
	Imbolc
	Magickal Focus:_____
	Daily Affirmation:_____
	_____
	Reflective Journal Keywords:_____
	_____
2nd SUNDAY	**To do**
Magickal Focus:_____	
Daily Affirmation:_____	
_____	
Reflective Journal Keywords:_____	
_____	

February 2025

3rd MONDAY	4th TUESDAY
Magickal Focus: _____ Daily Affirmation: _____ _____ Reflective Journal Keywords: _____ _____	Magickal Focus: _____ Daily Affirmation: _____ _____ Reflective Journal Keywords: _____ _____
5th WEDNESDAY	**6th THURSDAY**
First Quarter Moon Magickal Focus: _____ Daily Affirmation: _____ _____ Reflective Journal Keywords: _____ _____	Magickal Focus: _____ Daily Affirmation: _____ _____ Reflective Journal Keywords: _____ _____

7th FRIDAY

Magickal Focus: _____

Daily Affirmation: _____
_____

Reflective Journal Keywords: _____
_____

8th SATURDAY

Magickal Focus: _____

Daily Affirmation: _____
_____

Reflective Journal Keywords: _____
_____

9th SUNDAY

Magickal Focus: _____

Daily Affirmation: _____
_____

Reflective Journal Keywords: _____
_____

To do

February 2025

10th MONDAY

Magickal Focus: _____

Daily Affirmation: _____
_____

Reflective Journal Keywords: _____
_____

11th TUESDAY

Magickal Focus: _____

Daily Affirmation: _____
_____

Reflective Journal Keywords: _____
_____

12th WEDNESDAY

Full Moon

Magickal Focus: _____

Daily Affirmation: _____
_____

Reflective Journal Keywords: _____
_____

13th THURSDAY

Magickal Focus: _____

Daily Affirmation: _____
_____

Reflective Journal Keywords: _____
_____

14th FRIDAY	15th SATURDAY
Magickal Focus: _____ Daily Affirmation: _____ _____ Reflective Journal Keywords: _____ _____	Magickal Focus: _____ Daily Affirmation: _____ _____ Reflective Journal Keywords: _____ _____
16th SUNDAY	**To do**
Magickal Focus: _____ Daily Affirmation: _____ _____ Reflective Journal Keywords: _____ _____	

February 2025

17th MONDAY	18th TUESDAY
Magickal Focus: _____ Daily Affirmation: _____ _____ Reflective Journal Keywords: _____ _____	Magickal Focus: _____ Daily Affirmation: _____ _____ Reflective Journal Keywords: _____ _____
19th WEDNESDAY	**20th THURSDAY**
	Last Quarter Moon
Magickal Focus: _____ Daily Affirmation: _____ _____ Reflective Journal Keywords: _____ _____	Magickal Focus: _____ Daily Affirmation: _____ _____ Reflective Journal Keywords: _____ _____

21st FRIDAY

Magickal Focus: _____

Daily Affirmation: _____

_____

Reflective Journal Keywords: _____

_____

22nd SATURDAY

Magickal Focus: _____

Daily Affirmation: _____

_____

Reflective Journal Keywords: _____

_____

23rd SUNDAY

Magickal Focus: _____

Daily Affirmation: _____

_____

Reflective Journal Keywords: _____

_____

To do

February 2025

24th MONDAY	25th TUESDAY
Magickal Focus: _____ Daily Affirmation: _____ _____ Reflective Journal Keywords: _____ _____	Magickal Focus: _____ Daily Affirmation: _____ _____ Reflective Journal Keywords: _____ _____

26th WEDNESDAY	27th THURSDAY
● *Dark Moon* Magickal Focus: _____ Daily Affirmation: _____ _____ Reflective Journal Keywords: _____ _____	Magickal Focus: _____ Daily Affirmation: _____ _____ Reflective Journal Keywords: _____ _____

witchcraftspellsmagick.com

28th FRIDAY

Magickal Focus: _____

Daily Affirmation: _____

_____

Reflective Journal Keywords: _____

_____

NOTES

NOTES

To do

March 2025

Monday	Tuesday	Wednesday	Thursday	Friday
24	25	26	27	28
3	4	5	6 *First Quarter Moon*	7
10	11	12	13	14 *Full Moon in Virgo*
17	18	19	20 *Spring Equinox / Eostre*	21 *Last Quarter Moon*
24	25	26	27	28 *Dark Moon*
31	1	2	3	4

witchcraftspellsmagick.com

2025 Book of Shadows 115

Saturday	Sunday
1	2
8	9
15	16
22	23
29	30
5	6

This Month

Lunar Cycle Intention:
_____
_____

Most Important Events:
1. _____
2. _____
3. _____
4. _____
5. _____

To Do List:
○ _____
○ _____
○ _____
○ _____
○ _____
○ _____
○ _____

Notes & Thoughts:

March 2025

SPRING EQUINOX | ĒOSTRE - Lesser Witches' Sabbat
Ēostre is generally celebrated on the Spring Equinox, the 20th of March in the Northern Hemisphere and on the 23rd of September in the Southern Hemisphere.

The celebrations can span from the 19th to 23rd of March in the Northern Hemisphere and from the 19th to 23rd of September in the Southern Hemisphere. It celebrates the ancient Germanic goddess of spring, Eostre, also known as Eostar, Eastre, or Ēostre, who embodies transformative abilities and symbolizes the renewal of life with the arrival of spring.

During the Spring Equinox, Eostre's festival marks a moment of balance between night and day, echoing the harmony of nature. It is a time when seeds, once buried in the ground, begin to sprout anew, offering fresh starts and new beginnings as shoots emerge from the soil. This fruitful holiday is centered around the themes of rebirth, growth, and balance in nature, reminding us of the eternal cycles of life and the promise of rejuvenation that spring brings to all living things.

This Month's
RITUAL INSPIRATION

EOSTRE'S EGG HUNT - Celebrating the Goddess of Spring
Embark on a joyous and festive activity reminiscent of the ancient Ēostre rituals: the Egg Hunt. Hide decorated eggs, whether they be made of chocolate or hard-boiled, amidst the outdoor setting. Delight in the spirit of renewal and fertility as you partake in this playful celebration of the Goddess of Spring.

EMBRACE NATURE - Craft a Bee Haven and Sow Seeds for Abundance
Construct your own Bee Hive to honor the vital role of bees in nature. Craft a wooden box with an entrance and sloping roof for protection, then attach it to a fence. Provide nesting blocks to foster a sanctuary for these essential pollinators. Bless spring seeds for a bountiful season, aligning your efforts with the moon's phases for optimal growth. May your garden thrive with life and blessings.

witchcraftspellsmagick.com

Tarot Reading

Monthly Tarot readings offer you valuable guidance and insight for the month ahead. To start, shuffle your cards for at least 30-40 seconds while focusing on a specific question or area of your life that you would like guidance on.

When you're ready, lay down the top three cards to represent the past, present, and future. For further details on tarot, visit witchcraftspellsmagick.com

Past
Where you have been.

Current
Where you are now.

Future
Where you are going next.

Deck: _____ Date: _____

Card 1 - Past: _____

_____

_____

Card 2 - Current: _____

_____

_____

Card 3 - Future: _____

_____

_____

March Magickal Correspondences

During the Spring Equinox, Eostre's festival marks a moment of balance between night and day, echoing the harmony of nature and the renewal of life.

This is a time to celebrate growth, fertility, and new beginnings. The following correspondences are aligned with Eostre's energies and can be used in your magickal practices to enhance your connection with the season.

Animals - Bee, Butterfly, Horse, Lamb, Phoenix, Rabbit
Aromatics - Chamomile, Geranium, Lavender, Red Cedar, Sandalwood, Vetiver
Colors - Gold, Green, Pastel, White, Yellow
Crystals - Agate, Aquamarine, Bloodstone, Jade, Rose Quartz, Ruby
Flowers - Lilac, Narcissus, Peony, Rose, Tulip, Violet
Fruits - Apple, Cherry, Grapefruit, Lemon, Lime, Orange, Strawberry
Herbs - Basil, Lemon Verbena, Mint, Rosemary, Thyme
Spices - Cardamom, Cinnamon, Clove, Ginger, Nutmeg
Trees - Alder, Birch, Hawthorn, Pine, Willow

ALTAR CHECKLIST
Renewal, Balance + Growth
Altar Setup Basics - Start with the Elements:
Earth: Pentacle | Water: Chalice
Air: Incense or Diffuser | Fire: Candle

Additional Ideas:
- Eggs (actual or symbolic)
- Ribbons (decorate sticks with ribbons)
- Baskets (to hold nature's gifts, e.g., flowers)
- Plant buds (bless seeds before planting)
- Feathers | Nest/Cocoons
- Beeswax | Honeycomb
- Grains | Seeds
- Goddess (Maiden representation)
- Lemon cake | Honey cakes

Notes & Thoughts:

witchcraftspellsmagick.com

Sketch Your Altar Setup

Altar Planning

Creating a monthly altar helps you align with the cycles of nature and set focused intentions for your magickal practices.

Use this template to plan and organize your altar setup, ensuring that each element supports your intention and enhances your connection to the energies of the month. Thoughtful planning and intentional arrangement of your altar will amplify your magick and help manifest your desired outcomes.

Intention: _____

Desired Outcome: _____

Notable Monthly Energies: _____

_____

Altar Aesthetics: _____

_____

_____

Altar Elements: _____

_____

Intentions

Utilize an intention to form the foundation of your manifestation, which means creating the desired outcome in accordance with your will. Intentions are the purpose or reason for why you are creating a spell or engaging in any magickal practice.

This may be for love, good fortune, or to banish something from your life. When starting spell work, focus on intentions connected to yourself only, not others.

Even good magick can take on a life of its own and be unexpected, often tripling in power and energy and coming back to you —good, bad, or in a twisted form. When the time is right, choose as many intentions and cast as many protection charms, wellness, success, good fortune, and hope for love or companionship as you can manifest each month.

Intentions are woven into spells—spells hold the energy and the intention, working by following the path of least resistance. Start slow and small rather than aiming for unstoppable tidal waves.

Intention Setting

This month, choose 1-4 intentions to focus on, whether for the entire month, lunar cycle, or one per week, depending on how much you practice.

Setting clear and focused intentions is crucial in your magickal practice. Narrowing your focus helps channel your energy more effectively. Whether for self-improvement, attracting positivity, or banishing negativity, these intentions guide your magickal work and keep you aligned with your goals.

Review and select your intentions this month. Consistency and clarity are key, allowing your intentions to manifest through dedicated practice, repetition, effort, and willpower.

Adventure	Authenticity	Balance
Calm	Career	Change
Comfort	Communication	Community
Culture	Divine wisdom	Education
Energy	Family	Freedom
Friends	Fun	Growth
Happiness	Health	Honesty
Honoring	Integrity	Knowledge
Peace	Relationships	Resilience
Respect	Security	Self
Success	Travel	Trust
Wealth	Will	Wisdom

Spell Casting

TRANSFORM AN INTENTION INTO A SPELL

Crafting a spell involves careful planning and aligning various elements that resonate with your desired outcome.

Utilize spells to transform your intentions into reality. Use this template to plan and organize your spell work. Ensure each component supports and aligns with your intention, enhancing your magick with energy. By thoughtfully and mindfully selecting and arranging spell elements, you can amplify your magick and increase the effectiveness of your spell work. With focused intent and deliberate action, you will manifest your desires and achieve your goals.

Making Magick

When casting spells, consider which energies support your intention. Determine which correspondences, moon phases, planetary alignments, seasons, or times of day are best. Carefully selecting these elements enhances your spell's power and effectiveness.

Repetition Magick

Repetition Magick involves repeating your entire spell multiple times to strengthen the likelihood of achieving your desired outcome. This intensifies the energy and makes your spell more effective. **Never spell and tell before a spell has worked! It can muddle and redirect your focused energy, leading to negative results.**

Spell 1

Intention: _____

_____

Desired Outcome: _____

_____

_____

Correspondences: _____

_____

_____

_____

_____

_____

_____

witchcraftspellsmagick.com

Spell 2

Intention: _____

_____

Desired Outcome: _____

_____

_____

_____

Correspondences: _____

_____

_____

_____

_____

_____

_____

Spell 3

Intention: _____

_____

Desired Outcome: _____

_____

_____

_____

Correspondences: _____

_____

_____

_____

_____

_____

_____

Spells are the manifestation of your will!

Spells are a powerful tool for you to work with to manifest your desires. By setting a clear intention and casting a spell during a ritual, you can transform energy and bend outcomes to your will. These incantations, also known as enchantments or bewitchery, take many forms—spoken, written, thought, chanted, or sung. Successful spell work requires an alchemical mix of components and a lot of practice and patience. With dedication and focus, you can utilize the power of spells to create your desired outcome.

Ritual Preparation

SACRED SPACE AND CIRCLE CASTING STEPS

Cast a circle before spell and ritual work, or anytime you want to invoke protection and create a sacred space. Here are some steps to guide you:

1. Preparation
Collect objects and prepare your space for ritual or spell work.

2. Purification
Cleanse the space and yourself.

3. Casting
Create a physical or psychic circle for protection and manifestation.

4. Invocation
Introduce the energies you intend to work with. Invocation: *"I/we graciously invoke you..."*

5. Intention
Use your tool to draw a pentagram and state your intention.

6. Ritual Practice
Meditation, trance work, psychic divination, dance, chanting, spell work...

7. Closing
Dance, sing, or share offerings.

8. Gratitude and Reflection
Give thanks to the divine, metaphysical, elemental, spirit, and mortal energies you have worked with.

Ritual 1

Intention: _____

Desired Outcome: _____

Notable Monthly Energies: _____

_____

Altar Aesthetics: _____

_____

Altar Elements: _____

_____

Ritual 2

Intention: _____

Desired Outcome: _____

Notable Monthly Energies: _____

_____

Altar Aesthetics: _____

_____

Altar Elements: _____

_____

_____

1. Preparation, 2. Purification, 3. Casting, 4. Invocation,
5. Intention, 6. Ritual Practice, 7. Closing, 8. Gratitude and Reflection

Ritual 3

Intention: _____

Desired Outcome: _____

Notable Monthly Energies: _____

_____

Altar Aesthetics: _____

_____

Altar Elements: _____

_____

_____

March 2025

NOTES	1st SATURDAY
	Magickal Focus:_____ Daily Affirmation:_____ _____ Reflective Journal Keywords:_____ _____
2nd SUNDAY	**To do**
Magickal Focus:_____ Daily Affirmation:_____ _____ Reflective Journal Keywords:_____ _____	

March 2025

3rd MONDAY

Magickal Focus: _____

Daily Affirmation: _____
_____

Reflective Journal Keywords: _____
_____

4th TUESDAY

Magickal Focus: _____

Daily Affirmation: _____
_____

Reflective Journal Keywords: _____
_____

5th WEDNESDAY

Magickal Focus: _____

Daily Affirmation: _____
_____

Reflective Journal Keywords: _____
_____

6th THURSDAY

First Quarter Moon

Magickal Focus: _____

Daily Affirmation: _____
_____

Reflective Journal Keywords: _____
_____

7th FRIDAY

Magickal Focus: _____

Daily Affirmation: _____
_____

Reflective Journal Keywords: _____
_____

8th SATURDAY

Magickal Focus: _____

Daily Affirmation: _____
_____

Reflective Journal Keywords: _____
_____

9th SUNDAY

Magickal Focus: _____

Daily Affirmation: _____
_____

Reflective Journal Keywords: _____
_____

To do

March 2025

10th MONDAY	**11th TUESDAY**
Magickal Focus: _____ Daily Affirmation: _____ _____ Reflective Journal Keywords: _____ _____	Magickal Focus: _____ Daily Affirmation: _____ _____ Reflective Journal Keywords: _____ _____
12th WEDNESDAY	**13th THURSDAY**
Magickal Focus: _____ Daily Affirmation: _____ _____ Reflective Journal Keywords: _____ _____	Magickal Focus: _____ Daily Affirmation: _____ _____ Reflective Journal Keywords: _____ _____

14th FRIDAY

Full Moon

Magickal Focus: _____

Daily Affirmation: _____

_____

Reflective Journal Keywords: _____

_____

15th SATURDAY

Magickal Focus: _____

Daily Affirmation: _____

_____

Reflective Journal Keywords: _____

_____

16th SUNDAY

Magickal Focus: _____

Daily Affirmation: _____

_____

Reflective Journal Keywords: _____

_____

To do

March 2025

17th MONDAY

Magickal Focus: _____

Daily Affirmation: _____
_____

Reflective Journal Keywords: _____
_____

18th TUESDAY

Magickal Focus: _____

Daily Affirmation: _____
_____

Reflective Journal Keywords: _____
_____

19th WEDNESDAY

Magickal Focus: _____

Daily Affirmation: _____
_____

Reflective Journal Keywords: _____
_____

20th THURSDAY

Spring Equinox
Ēostre

Magickal Focus: _____

Daily Affirmation: _____
_____

Reflective Journal Keywords: _____
_____

witchcraftspellsmagick.com

21st FRIDAY

Last Quarter Moon

Magickal Focus: _____

Daily Affirmation: _____

_____

Reflective Journal Keywords: _____

_____

22nd SATURDAY

Magickal Focus: _____

Daily Affirmation: _____

_____

Reflective Journal Keywords: _____

_____

23rd SUNDAY

Magickal Focus: _____

Daily Affirmation: _____

_____

Reflective Journal Keywords: _____

_____

To do

March 2025

24th MONDAY	25th TUESDAY
Magickal Focus: _____ Daily Affirmation: _____ _____ Reflective Journal Keywords: _____ _____	Magickal Focus: _____ Daily Affirmation: _____ _____ Reflective Journal Keywords: _____ _____
26th WEDNESDAY	**27th THURSDAY**
Magickal Focus: _____ Daily Affirmation: _____ _____ Reflective Journal Keywords: _____ _____	Magickal Focus: _____ Daily Affirmation: _____ _____ Reflective Journal Keywords: _____ _____

28th FRIDAY

● *Dark Moon*

Magickal Focus: _____

Daily Affirmation: _____

_____

Reflective Journal Keywords: _____

_____

29th SATURDAY

Magickal Focus: _____

Daily Affirmation: _____

_____

Reflective Journal Keywords: _____

_____

30th SUNDAY

Magickal Focus: _____

Daily Affirmation: _____

_____

Reflective Journal Keywords: _____

_____

To do

March 2025

31st MONDAY

Magickal Focus: _____

Daily Affirmation: _____

_____

Reflective Journal Keywords: _____

_____

NOTES

NOTES

To do

April 2025

Monday	Tuesday	Wednesday	Thursday	Friday
31	1	2	3	4 *First Quarter Moon*
7	8	9	10	11
14	15	16	17	18
21	22	23	24	25
28	29	30 *Beltane*	1 *Beltane*	2
5	6	7	8	9

witchcraftspellsmagick.com

2025 Book of Shadows   139

Saturday	Sunday
5	6
12　*Full Moon in Libra*	13
19	20　*Last Quarter Moon*
26　*Dark Moon*	27
3	4
10	11

This Month

Lunar Cycle Intention:

_____

_____

Most Important Events:

1. _____
2. _____
3. _____
4. _____
5. _____

To Do List:

○ _____
○ _____
○ _____
○ _____
○ _____
○ _____
○ _____

Notes & Thoughts:

April 2025

BELTANE - Greater Witches' Sabbat

Beltane, or Bealtaine, is observed from the 30th of April to the 1st of May in the Northern Hemisphere and from the 31st of October to the 1st of November in the Southern Hemisphere.

Traditionally, special bonfires are kindled, with flames, smoke, and ashes sending out protective energies. As the seasons shift, so too does our approach to magick. Mindfully reflecting on the changing energies can greatly enhance our witchcraft practice. With longer and warmer days, we move closer to the Summer Solstice. This time of year witnesses the beauty of new growth as trees and flowers blossom, birds and insects sing, and life flourishes around us. Beltane is often a time for relationship rituals, such as handfasting for joining and handparting for endings. Modern witches see the fertility aspect of Beltane as a time to birth new ideas and renew both body and soul. Embracing these energies, we welcome the promise of growth and transformation that Beltane brings.

This Month's
RITUAL INSPIRATION
GREEN MAN - Spirit of the Forest

A symbol of rebirth, and the cycle of new growth of spring. The Green Man may take any form, naturalistic or decorative, made from leaves, branches, and foliage. Place him on your Beltane altar to honor the renewing forces of nature.

WITCH'S WAND - Craft Lore

Craft and decorate a found stick, carve or paint, tie ribbons, charms, or bells. Use your wand to direct energy and cast spells, enhancing your magickal practice during Beltane.

FLORAL CROWNS - Ritual Adornment

A symbol of fertility, love, and celebration, popular throughout history. Wear them during your Beltane rituals to embody the vibrant energy of the season.

witchcraftspellsmagick.com

Tarot Reading

Monthly Tarot readings offer you valuable guidance and insight for the month ahead. To start, shuffle your cards for at least 30-40 seconds while focusing on a specific question or area of your life that you would like guidance on.

When you're ready, lay down the top three cards to represent the past, present, and future. For further details on tarot, visit witchcraftspellsmagick.com

Past *Where you have been.*	**Current** *Where you are now.*	**Future** *Where you are going next.*

Deck: _____ **Date:** _____

Card 1 - Past: _____

_____

_____

Card 2 - Current: _____

_____

_____

Card 3 - Future: _____

_____

_____

April Magickal Correspondences

April offers energies of transformation and renewal as nature awakens and flourishes. Longer, warmer days symbolize balance and the promise of growth.

With Beltane at month's end, marking peak fertility, it's the perfect time for magick focused on fortune and purification. Below are correspondences to inspire your monthly altar and align with April's energies.

Animals - Bee, Deer, Dove, Frog, Rabbit, Stang
Aromatics - Dragon's Blood, Frankincense, Myrrh, Patchouli, Rose, Ylang-ylang
Colours - Green, Orange, Pink, Purple, Red, White
Crystals - Amethyst, Citrine, Emerald, Fire agate, Rose quartz, Turquoise
Flowers - Daisy, Dandelion, Jasmine, Marigold, Pansy, Sunflower, Violet
Fruits -Apple, Berry, Lemon, Peach, Plum
Herbs - Basil, Dill, Lemon balm, Mint, Mugwort, Rosemary, Rue, Sage, Thyme
Spices - Chili, Cinnamon, Clove, Nutmeg, Paprika, Saffron
Trees -Birch, Cedar, Hawthorn, Maple, Oak, Rowan, Willow

ALTAR CHECKLIST

Fortune + Purification

Altar Setup Basics - Start with the Elements:
Earth: Pentacle | Water: Chalice
Air: Incense or Diffuser | Fire: Candle

Additional Ideas:
- Maypole
- Ribbons
- Foliage/Greenery
- Shaman Drum/Ribbons/Bells
- Coins | Horseshoes | Clover (for Fortune)
- Salt | Sage | Water (for Purification)
- Basket of flowers/Bowl of Sunflower seeds
- Garlands | Wreath | Sticks
- Antlers (for Strength and Natural cycles)

Notes & Thoughts:

witchcraftspellsmagick.com

[Sketch Your Altar Setup]

Altar Planning

Creating a monthly altar helps you align with the cycles of nature and set focused intentions for your magickal practices.

Use this template to plan and organize your altar setup, ensuring that each element supports your intention and enhances your connection to the energies of the month. Thoughtful planning and intentional arrangement of your altar will amplify your magick and help manifest your desired outcomes.

Intention: _____

Desired Outcome: _____

Notable Monthly Energies: _____

_____

Altar Aesthetics: _____

_____

_____

Altar Elements: _____

_____

Intentions

Utilize an intention to form the foundation of your manifestation, which means creating the desired outcome in accordance with your will. Intentions are the purpose or reason for why you are creating a spell or engaging in any magickal practice.

This may be for love, good fortune, or to banish something from your life. When starting spell work, focus on intentions connected to yourself only, not others.

Even good magick can take on a life of its own and be unexpected, often tripling in power and energy and coming back to you —good, bad, or in a twisted form. When the time is right, choose as many intentions and cast as many protection charms, wellness, success, good fortune, and hope for love or companionship as you can manifest each month.

Intentions are woven into spells—spells hold the energy and the intention, working by following the path of least resistance. Start slow and small rather than aiming for unstoppable tidal waves.

Intention Setting

This month, choose 1-4 intentions to focus on, whether for the entire month, lunar cycle, or one per week, depending on how much you practice.

Setting clear and focused intentions is crucial in your magickal practice. Narrowing your focus helps channel your energy more effectively. Whether for self-improvement, attracting positivity, or banishing negativity, these intentions guide your magickal work and keep you aligned with your goals.

Review and select your intentions this month. Consistency and clarity are key, allowing your intentions to manifest through dedicated practice, repetition, effort, and willpower.

Adventure	Authenticity	Balance
Calm	Career	Change
Comfort	Communication	Community
Culture	Divine wisdom	Education
Energy	Family	Freedom
Friends	Fun	Growth
Happiness	Health	Honesty
Honoring	Integrity	Knowledge
Peace	Relationships	Resilience
Respect	Security	Self
Success	Travel	Trust
Wealth	Will	Wisdom

Spell Casting

TRANSFORM AN INTENTION INTO A SPELL

Crafting a spell involves careful planning and aligning various elements that resonate with your desired outcome.

Utilize spells to transform your intentions into reality. Use this template to plan and organize your spell work. Ensure each component supports and aligns with your intention, enhancing your magick with energy. By thoughtfully and mindfully selecting and arranging spell elements, you can amplify your magick and increase the effectiveness of your spell work. With focused intent and deliberate action, you will manifest your desires and achieve your goals.

Making Magick

When casting spells, consider which energies support your intention. Determine which correspondences, moon phases, planetary alignments, seasons, or times of day are best. Carefully selecting these elements enhances your spell's power and effectiveness.

Repetition Magick

Repetition Magick involves repeating your entire spell multiple times to strengthen the likelihood of achieving your desired outcome. This intensifies the energy and makes your spell more effective. **Never spell and tell before a spell has worked! It can muddle and redirect your focused energy, leading to negative results.**

Spell 1

Intention: _____

_____

Desired Outcome: _____

_____

_____

_____

Correspondences: _____

_____

_____

_____

_____

_____

_____

_____

witchcraftspellsmagick.com

Spell 2

Intention: _____

_____

Desired Outcome: _____

_____

_____

_____

Correspondences: _____

_____

_____

_____

_____

_____

_____

Spell 3

Intention: _____

_____

Desired Outcome: _____

_____

_____

_____

Correspondences: _____

_____

_____

_____

_____

_____

_____

Spells are the manifestation of your will!

Spells are a powerful tool for you to work with to manifest your desires.
By setting a clear intention and casting a spell during a ritual,
you can transform energy and bend outcomes to your will.
These incantations, also known as enchantments or bewitchery,
take many forms—spoken, written, thought, chanted, or sung.
Successful spell work requires an alchemical mix of components
and a lot of practice and patience. With dedication and focus,
you can utilize the power of spells to create your desired outcome.

Ritual Preparation

SACRED SPACE AND CIRCLE CASTING STEPS

Cast a circle before spell and ritual work, or anytime you want to invoke protection and create a sacred space. Here are some steps to guide you:

1. Preparation
Collect objects and prepare your space for ritual or spell work.

2. Purification
Cleanse the space and yourself.

3. Casting
Create a physical or psychic circle for protection and manifestation.

4. Invocation
Introduce the energies you intend to work with. Invocation: *"I/we graciously invoke you..."*

5. Intention
Use your tool to draw a pentagram and state your intention.

6. Ritual Practice
Meditation, trance work, psychic divination, dance, chanting, spell work...

7. Closing
Dance, sing, or share offerings.

8. Gratitude and Reflection
Give thanks to the divine, metaphysical, elemental, spirit, and mortal energies you have worked with.

Ritual 1

Intention: _____

Desired Outcome: _____

Notable Monthly Energies: _____

_____

Altar Aesthetics: _____

_____

Altar Elements: _____

_____

_____

Ritual 2

Intention: _____

Desired Outcome: _____

Notable Monthly Energies: _____

_____

Altar Aesthetics: _____

_____

Altar Elements: _____

_____

_____

1. Preparation, 2. Purification, 3. Casting, 4. Invocation,
5. Intention, 6. Ritual Practice, 7. Closing, 8. Gratitude and Reflection

Ritual 3

Intention: _____

Desired Outcome: _____

Notable Monthly Energies: _____

_____

Altar Aesthetics: _____

_____

Altar Elements: _____

_____

_____

April 2025

To do	1st TUESDAY
	Magickal Focus:_____ Daily Affirmation: _____ _____ Reflective Journal Keywords: _____ _____
2nd WEDNESDAY	**3rd THURSDAY**
Magickal Focus:_____ Daily Affirmation: _____ _____ Reflective Journal Keywords: _____ _____	Magickal Focus:_____ Daily Affirmation: _____ _____ Reflective Journal Keywords: _____ _____

witchcraftspellsmagick.com

4th FRIDAY *First Quarter Moon* Magickal Focus:_____ Daily Affirmation: _____ _____ Reflective Journal Keywords: _____ _____	**5th SATURDAY** Magickal Focus:_____ Daily Affirmation: _____ _____ Reflective Journal Keywords: _____ _____
6th SUNDAY Magickal Focus:_____ Daily Affirmation: _____ _____ Reflective Journal Keywords: _____ _____	**To do**

April 2025

7th MONDAY	8th TUESDAY
Magickal Focus: _____ Daily Affirmation: _____ _____ Reflective Journal Keywords: _____ _____	Magickal Focus: _____ Daily Affirmation: _____ _____ Reflective Journal Keywords: _____ _____
9th WEDNESDAY	**10th THURSDAY**
Magickal Focus: _____ Daily Affirmation: _____ _____ Reflective Journal Keywords: _____ _____	Magickal Focus: _____ Daily Affirmation: _____ _____ Reflective Journal Keywords: _____ _____

11th FRIDAY

Magickal Focus: _____

Daily Affirmation: _____

_____

Reflective Journal Keywords: _____

_____

12th SATURDAY

Full Moon

Magickal Focus: _____

Daily Affirmation: _____

_____

Reflective Journal Keywords: _____

_____

13th SUNDAY

Magickal Focus: _____

Daily Affirmation: _____

_____

Reflective Journal Keywords: _____

_____

To do

April 2025

14th MONDAY	15th TUESDAY
Magickal Focus: _____ Daily Affirmation: _____ _____ Reflective Journal Keywords: _____ _____	Magickal Focus: _____ Daily Affirmation: _____ _____ Reflective Journal Keywords: _____ _____
16th WEDNESDAY	**17th THURSDAY**
Magickal Focus: _____ Daily Affirmation: _____ _____ Reflective Journal Keywords: _____ _____	Magickal Focus: _____ Daily Affirmation: _____ _____ Reflective Journal Keywords: _____ _____

18th FRIDAY	19th SATURDAY
Magickal Focus: _____	Magickal Focus: _____
Daily Affirmation: _____	Daily Affirmation: _____
Reflective Journal Keywords: _____	Reflective Journal Keywords: _____
20th SUNDAY *Last Quarter Moon*	**To do**
Magickal Focus: _____	
Daily Affirmation: _____	
Reflective Journal Keywords: _____	

April 2025

21st MONDAY	22nd TUESDAY
Magickal Focus: _____ Daily Affirmation: _____ _____ Reflective Journal Keywords: _____ _____	Magickal Focus: _____ Daily Affirmation: _____ _____ Reflective Journal Keywords: _____ _____
23rd WEDNESDAY	**24th THURSDAY**
Magickal Focus: _____ Daily Affirmation: _____ _____ Reflective Journal Keywords: _____ _____	Magickal Focus: _____ Daily Affirmation: _____ _____ Reflective Journal Keywords: _____ _____

witchcraftspellsmagick.com

25th FRIDAY

Magickal Focus: _____

Daily Affirmation: _____

_____

Reflective Journal Keywords: _____

_____

26th SATURDAY

Dark Moon

Magickal Focus: _____

Daily Affirmation: _____

_____

Reflective Journal Keywords: _____

_____

27th SUNDAY

Magickal Focus: _____

Daily Affirmation: _____

_____

Reflective Journal Keywords: _____

_____

To do

April 2025

28th MONDAY	29th TUESDAY
Magickal Focus: _____	Magickal Focus: _____
Daily Affirmation: _____	Daily Affirmation: _____
Reflective Journal Keywords: _____	Reflective Journal Keywords: _____

30th WEDNESDAY	To do
Beltane Magickal Focus: _____ Daily Affirmation: _____ Reflective Journal Keywords: _____	

witchcraftspellsmagick.com

May 2025

Monday	Tuesday	Wednesday	Thursday	Friday
28	29	30 *Beltane*	1 *Beltane*	2
5	6	7	8	9
12 *Full Moon in Scorpio*	13	14	15	16
19 *Last Quarter Moon*	20	21	22	23
26	27	28	29	30
2	3	4	5	6

witchcraftspellsmagick.com

2025 Book of Shadows   161

Saturday	Sunday
3	4
	First Quarter Moon
10	11
17	18
24	25
	Dark Moon
31	1
7	8

This Month

Lunar Cycle Intention:
_____
_____

Most Important Events:
1. _____
2. _____
3. _____
4. _____
5. _____

To Do List:
○ _____
○ _____
○ _____
○ _____
○ _____
○ _____
○ _____

Notes & Thoughts:

May 2025

MOON ESBAT - Witches' Sabbat

The May Full Moon is observed on the 12th in the Northern Hemisphere and the 13th in the Southern Hemisphere, is a sacred celebration focused on connecting with the Triple Goddess.

Witches' Esbats are monthly gatherings held during the full moon, offering an opportunity for practitioners to deepen their connection with lunar energies. These gatherings honor the phases of the moon, with the Maiden representing the new moon, the Mother the full moon, and the Crone the waning moon.

Esbats provide an opportunity to practice and connect in between Sabbats. During a full moon, emotions may be heightened, so it's important to be mindful of making decisions based on rational thinking rather than irrational thoughts. Despite the intensity, a full moon serves as nature's way of waking you up from everyday life and tipping your world on its head. The moon, a symbol of femininity, offers a perfect opportunity for sharing, teaching, healing, and learning. Esbats provide a different energy than Sabbats, helping to create a harmonious balance in your practice.

This Month's RITUAL INSPIRATION

HONOR WITH GRATITUDE - Healing and Growth Ceremony

Honor with gratitude - Healing and Growth Ceremony
Hold a ritual ceremony to honor nature's gifts during the May Moon Esbat.
Counterbalance the cosmic energy with tangible elements of nature.

MOON WATER - Re-energizing Nourishing Energy

Place a glass jar of pure water under the May full moon.
Use the collected Moon Water to cleanse crystals, add
to your bath, or brew in tea for nourishment and renewal.

FLOWER OFFERINGS - Nature's Tribute

Gather fresh flowers and create small bouquets. Offer these to the earth, rivers, or sacred spaces as a tribute to nature's beauty and abundance during the May Moon Esbat.

witchcraftspellsmagick.com

Tarot Reading

Monthly Tarot readings offer you valuable guidance and insight for the month ahead. To start, shuffle your cards for at least 30-40 seconds while focusing on a specific question or area of your life that you would like guidance on.

When you're ready, lay down the top three cards to represent the past, present, and future. For further details on tarot, visit witchcraftspellsmagick.com

Past	**Current**	**Future**
Where you have been.	*Where you are now.*	*Where you are going next.*

Deck: _____ Date: _____

Card 1 - Past: _____

_____

_____

Card 2 - Current: _____

_____

_____

Card 3 - Future: _____

_____

_____

May Magickal Correspondences

May ushers in a time of vibrant growth and blooming potential, a month where the energies of spring are in full swing.

The days grow longer and warmer, encouraging the flourishing of life and creativity. This month is ideal for focusing on the Moon Esbat, celebrating the cycles of the moon and the deep connection between lunar energies and your magickal practices.

Animals - Bat, Bee, Butterfly, Dove, Frog, Owl, Rabbit, Wolf
Aromatics - Jasmine, Lilac, Rose, Sage, Sandalwood, Sweetgrass
Colours - Silver, White, Pale Blue, Purple
Crystals - Clear quartz, Emerald, Jade, Malachite, Moonstone
Flowers - Daisy, Hawthorn, Night-Blooming Jasmine, Peony, Rose, White Roses
Fruits - Apple, Cherry, Strawberry, Blueberry, Lemon, Orange
Herbs - Basil, Elderflower, Mint, Mugwort, Thyme
Spices - Cinnamon, Clove, Ginger
Trees - Hawthorn, Maple, Oak, Rowan, Willow

ALTAR CHECKLIST
Moon Esbat
Altar Setup Basics - Start with the Elements:
Earth: Pentacle | Water: Chalice
Air: Incense or Diffuser | Fire: Candle

Additional Ideas:
- Full moon symbol | Moon Goddess statue
- Fresh flowers (Lilac, Lily of the Valley)
- Moon water
- Herbs (Mugwort, Lavender)
- Ritual bowl | Symbols of growth
- Silver jewelry | Feathers
- Offerings (Milk, Honey)
- Journal or Book of Shadows
- Mirror | White cloth (altar covering)

Notes & Thoughts:

Sketch Your Altar Setup

Altar Planning

Creating a monthly altar helps you align with the cycles of nature and set focused intentions for your magickal practices.

Use this template to plan and organize your altar setup, ensuring that each element supports your intention and enhances your connection to the energies of the month. Thoughtful planning and intentional arrangement of your altar will amplify your magick and help manifest your desired outcomes.

Intention: _____

Desired Outcome: _____

Notable Monthly Energies: _____

_____

Altar Aesthetics: _____

_____

_____

Altar Elements: _____

_____

Intentions

Utilize an intention to form the foundation of your manifestation, which means creating the desired outcome in accordance with your will. Intentions are the purpose or reason for why you are creating a spell or engaging in any magickal practice.

This may be for love, good fortune, or to banish something from your life. When starting spell work, focus on intentions connected to yourself only, not others.

Even good magick can take on a life of its own and be unexpected, often tripling in power and energy and coming back to you —good, bad, or in a twisted form. When the time is right, choose as many intentions and cast as many protection charms, wellness, success, good fortune, and hope for love or companionship as you can manifest each month.

Intentions are woven into spells—spells hold the energy and the intention, working by following the path of least resistance. Start slow and small rather than aiming for unstoppable tidal waves.

Intention Setting

This month, choose 1-4 intentions to focus on, whether for the entire month, lunar cycle, or one per week, depending on how much you practice.

Setting clear and focused intentions is crucial in your magickal practice. Narrowing your focus helps channel your energy more effectively. Whether for self-improvement, attracting positivity, or banishing negativity, these intentions guide your magickal work and keep you aligned with your goals.

Review and select your intentions this month. Consistency and clarity are key, allowing your intentions to manifest through dedicated practice, repetition, effort, and willpower.

Adventure	Authenticity	Balance
Calm	Career	Change
Comfort	Communication	Community
Culture	Divine wisdom	Education
Energy	Family	Freedom
Friends	Fun	Growth
Happiness	Health	Honesty
Honoring	Integrity	Knowledge
Peace	Relationships	Resilience
Respect	Security	Self
Success	Travel	Trust
Wealth	Will	Wisdom

Spell Casting
TRANSFORM AN INTENTION INTO A SPELL

Crafting a spell involves careful planning and aligning various elements that resonate with your desired outcome.

Utilize spells to transform your intentions into reality. Use this template to plan and organize your spell work. Ensure each component supports and aligns with your intention, enhancing your magick with energy. By thoughtfully and mindfully selecting and arranging spell elements, you can amplify your magick and increase the effectiveness of your spell work. With focused intent and deliberate action, you will manifest your desires and achieve your goals.

Making Magick

When casting spells, consider which energies support your intention. Determine which correspondences, moon phases, planetary alignments, seasons, or times of day are best. Carefully selecting these elements enhances your spell's power and effectiveness.

Repetition Magick

Repetition Magick involves repeating your entire spell multiple times to strengthen the likelihood of achieving your desired outcome. This intensifies the energy and makes your spell more effective. **Never spell and tell before a spell has worked! It can muddle and redirect your focused energy, leading to negative results.**

Spell 1

Intention: _____

_____

Desired Outcome: _____

_____

_____

_____

Correspondences: _____

_____

_____

_____

_____

_____

_____

witchcraftspellsmagick.com

Spell 2

Intention: _____

_____

Desired Outcome: _____

_____

_____

_____

Correspondences: _____

_____

_____

_____

_____

_____

Spell 3

Intention: _____

_____

Desired Outcome: _____

_____

_____

_____

Correspondences: _____

_____

_____

_____

_____

_____

Spells are the manifestation of your will!

Spells are a powerful tool for you to work with to manifest your desires. By setting a clear intention and casting a spell during a ritual, you can transform energy and bend outcomes to your will. These incantations, also known as enchantments or bewitchery, take many forms—spoken, written, thought, chanted, or sung. Successful spell work requires an alchemical mix of components and a lot of practice and patience. With dedication and focus, you can utilize the power of spells to create your desired outcome.

Ritual Preparation

SACRED SPACE AND CIRCLE CASTING STEPS

Cast a circle before spell and ritual work, or anytime you want to invoke protection and create a sacred space. Here are some steps to guide you:

1. Preparation
Collect objects and prepare your space for ritual or spell work.

2. Purification
Cleanse the space and yourself.

3. Casting
Create a physical or psychic circle for protection and manifestation.

4. Invocation
Introduce the energies you intend to work with. Invocation: *"I/we graciously invoke you..."*

5. Intention
Use your tool to draw a pentagram and state your intention.

6. Ritual Practice
Meditation, trance work, psychic divination, dance, chanting, spell work...

7. Closing
Dance, sing, or share offerings.

8. Gratitude and Reflection
Give thanks to the divine, metaphysical, elemental, spirit, and mortal energies you have worked with.

Ritual 1

Intention: _____

Desired Outcome: _____

Notable Monthly Energies: _____

_____

Altar Aesthetics: _____

_____

Altar Elements: _____

_____

_____

witchcraftspellsmagick.com

Ritual 2

Intention: _____

Desired Outcome: _____

Notable Monthly Energies: _____

_____

Altar Aesthetics: _____

_____

Altar Elements: _____

_____

_____

---

1. Preparation, 2. Purification, 3. Casting, 4. Invocation,
5. Intention, 6. Ritual Practice, 7. Closing, 8. Gratitude and Reflection

---

Ritual 3

Intention: _____

Desired Outcome: _____

Notable Monthly Energies: _____

_____

Altar Aesthetics: _____

_____

Altar Elements: _____

_____

_____

May 2025

NOTES	To do
	Magickal Focus: _____
	Daily Affirmation: _____
	Reflective Journal Keywords: _____

To do	1st THURSDAY
	Beltane
Magickal Focus: _____	Magickal Focus: _____
Daily Affirmation: _____	Daily Affirmation: _____
Reflective Journal Keywords: _____	Reflective Journal Keywords: _____

2nd FRIDAY	3rd SATURDAY
Magickal Focus: _____ Daily Affirmation: _____ _____ Reflective Journal Keywords: _____ _____	Magickal Focus: _____ Daily Affirmation: _____ _____ Reflective Journal Keywords: _____ _____
4th SUNDAY	To do
First Quarter Moon Magickal Focus: _____ Daily Affirmation: _____ _____ Reflective Journal Keywords: _____ _____	

May 2025

5th MONDAY

Magickal Focus: _____

Daily Affirmation: _____
_____

Reflective Journal Keywords: _____
_____

6th TUESDAY

Magickal Focus: _____

Daily Affirmation: _____
_____

Reflective Journal Keywords: _____
_____

7th WEDNESDAY

Magickal Focus: _____

Daily Affirmation: _____
_____

Reflective Journal Keywords: _____
_____

8th THURSDAY

Magickal Focus: _____

Daily Affirmation: _____
_____

Reflective Journal Keywords: _____
_____

witchcraftspellsmagick.com

9th FRIDAY	**10th SATURDAY**
Magickal Focus: _____	Magickal Focus: _____
Daily Affirmation: _____	Daily Affirmation: _____
Reflective Journal Keywords: _____	Reflective Journal Keywords: _____
11th SUNDAY	**To do**
Magickal Focus: _____	
Daily Affirmation: _____	
Reflective Journal Keywords: _____	

May 2025

12th MONDAY	13th TUESDAY
Full Moon Magickal Focus: _____ Daily Affirmation: _____ _____ Reflective Journal Keywords: _____ _____	 Magickal Focus: _____ Daily Affirmation: _____ _____ Reflective Journal Keywords: _____ _____
14th WEDNESDAY	**15th THURSDAY**
     Magickal Focus: _____ Daily Affirmation: _____ _____ Reflective Journal Keywords: _____ _____	 Magickal Focus: _____ Daily Affirmation: _____ _____ Reflective Journal Keywords: _____ _____

16th FRIDAY

Magickal Focus: _____

Daily Affirmation: _____

_____

Reflective Journal Keywords: _____

_____

17th SATURDAY

Magickal Focus: _____

Daily Affirmation: _____

_____

Reflective Journal Keywords: _____

_____

18th SUNDAY

Magickal Focus: _____

Daily Affirmation: _____

_____

Reflective Journal Keywords: _____

_____

To do

May 2025

19th MONDAY	20th TUESDAY
Last Quarter Moon Magickal Focus: _____ Daily Affirmation: _____ _____ Reflective Journal Keywords: _____ _____	 Magickal Focus: _____ Daily Affirmation: _____ _____ Reflective Journal Keywords: _____ _____
21st WEDNESDAY	**22nd THURSDAY**
     Magickal Focus: _____ Daily Affirmation: _____ _____ Reflective Journal Keywords: _____ _____	 Magickal Focus: _____ Daily Affirmation: _____ _____ Reflective Journal Keywords: _____ _____

witchcraftspellsmagick.com

2025 Book of Shadows   179

23rd FRIDAY

Magickal Focus: _____

Daily Affirmation: _____

_____

Reflective Journal Keywords: _____

_____

24th SATURDAY

Magickal Focus: _____

Daily Affirmation: _____

_____

Reflective Journal Keywords: _____

_____

25th SUNDAY

●
Dark Moon

Magickal Focus: _____

Daily Affirmation: _____

_____

Reflective Journal Keywords: _____

_____

To do

May 2025

26th MONDAY

Magickal Focus: _____

Daily Affirmation: _____
_____

Reflective Journal Keywords: _____
_____

27th TUESDAY

Magickal Focus: _____

Daily Affirmation: _____
_____

Reflective Journal Keywords: _____
_____

28th WEDNESDAY

Magickal Focus: _____

Daily Affirmation: _____
_____

Reflective Journal Keywords: _____
_____

29th THURSDAY

Magickal Focus: _____

Daily Affirmation: _____
_____

Reflective Journal Keywords: _____
_____

witchcraftspellsmagick.com

30th FRIDAY	**31st SATURDAY**
Magickal Focus:_____	Magickal Focus:_____
Daily Affirmation:_____	Daily Affirmation:_____
Reflective Journal Keywords:_____	Reflective Journal Keywords:_____
NOTES	**To do**

June 2025

Monday	Tuesday	Wednesday	Thursday	Friday
26	27	28	29	30
2 *First Quarter Moon*	3	4	5	6
9	10 *Full Moon in Sagittarius*	11	12	13
16	17 *Last Quarter Moon*	18	19	20
23	24 *Dark Moon*	25	26	27
30	1	2	3	4

Saturday	Sunday
31	1
7	8
14	15
21 *Summer Solstice Litha*	22
28	29
5	6

This Month

Lunar Cycle Intention:

_____

_____

Most Important Events:

1. _____
2. _____
3. _____
4. _____
5. _____

To Do List:

○ _____
○ _____
○ _____
○ _____
○ _____
○ _____
○ _____

Notes & Thoughts:

June 2025

SUMMER SOLSTICE | LITHA - Lesser Witches' Sabbat
Summer Solstice and the Witches' Sabbat Litha are observed on the 21st of June in the Northern Hemisphere and the 21st of December in the Southern Hemisphere, is a sacred celebration marking the Summer Solstice.

This festival, also known as Midsummer, is the longest day of the year when the sun reaches its peak. The Summer Solstice is an ideal time to focus on energies of growth, abundance, love, gratitude, partnerships, and union. As we gather to celebrate Litha, we embrace the vibrant life that flourishes around us, reflecting on the transformative power of the sun and the perpetual cycle of nature.

Litha is also a time for honoring the elements and nature spirits. Creating sunwheels, decorating with flowers, and lighting bonfires are traditional ways to celebrate this Sabbat. It is a powerful opportunity to connect with the earth, express creativity, and set intentions for the months ahead. Many witches use this time to perform rituals that encourage personal growth, protection, and the manifestation of desires.

This Month's
RITUAL INSPIRATION

SUNCATCHER - Honoring the Sun
Fasten collected found sticks with natural hemp twine, and hang feathers, crystals, or bright glass beads from your suncatcher. This simple craft will help you honor the sun's energy during Litha, bringing light and beauty into your sacred space.

NATURE WALKS - Pagan Paths
Take nature walks to help you connect, relax, and recharge, offering the perfect opportunity to collect gifts for your altar.

LITHA WREATH - Handcrafted Adornment
Collect yellow, orange, and red brightly colored flowers to make a Litha wreath. This beautiful adornment symbolizes the peak of summer and can be placed on your door or altar to celebrate the abundant energy and warmth of Litha.

witchcraftspellsmagick.com

Tarot Reading

Monthly Tarot readings offer you valuable guidance and insight for the month ahead. To start, shuffle your cards for at least 30-40 seconds while focusing on a specific question or area of your life that you would like guidance on.

When you're ready, lay down the top three cards to represent the past, present, and future. For further details on tarot, visit witchcraftspellsmagick.com

Past
Where you have been.

Current
Where you are now.

Future
Where you are going next.

Deck: _____ **Date:** _____

Card 1 - Past: _____

_____

_____

Card 2 - Current: _____

_____

_____

Card 3 - Future: _____

_____

_____

June Magickal Correspondences

June heralds a time of vibrant energy and transformation as nature thrives under the long, warm days.

This month includes the celebration of Litha, the Summer Solstice, marking the peak of the sun's power and a moment of balance between light and dark. It's a time to honor growth, abundance, and the blessings of the sun.

Animals - Bee, Bull, Deer, Eagle, Frog, Hawk, Horse
Colours - Blue, Gold, Green, Orange, Pink, Purple, White, Yellow
Crystals - Amethyst, Carnelian, Citrine, Clear Quartz, Diamond, Jade, Tiger's Eye
Flowers - Daisy, Dandelion, Elderflower, Heather, Marigold, Poppy, Rose
Fruits - Apple, Berry, Grape, Lemon, Orange, Pear
Herbs - Basil, Foxglove, Mint, Sage, St John's Wort, Thyme, Yarrow
Aromatics - Eucalyptus, Geranium, Lavender, Mint, Patchouli, Rosemary, Vervain
Spices - Chilli, Cinnamon, Clove, Nutmeg
Trees - Birch, Elder, Hazel, Oak, Rowan, Willow

ALTAR CHECKLIST
Blessings of Sun
Altar Setup Basics - Start with the Elements:
Earth: Pentacle | Water: Chalice
Air: Incense or Diffuser | Fire: Candle

Additional Ideas:
- Emperor | Empress Tarot cards
- Honey | Honeycomb
- Roses, petals | Rosettes | Objects of love
- Sunflower seeds | Sunflowers
- Sun wheel | Symbols of the sun | Spirals
- Ritual basket | Colorful flowers
- Summer deities - Freya, Flora, Habondia
- Sun Gods - Ra, Sol, Lugh, Helios
- Feathers | Herbs | Citrus Fruits | Crystals

Notes & Thoughts:

witchcraftspellsmagick.com

Sketch Your Altar Setup

Altar Planning

Creating a monthly altar helps you align with the cycles of nature and set focused intentions for your magickal practices.

Use this template to plan and organize your altar setup, ensuring that each element supports your intention and enhances your connection to the energies of the month. Thoughtful planning and intentional arrangement of your altar will amplify your magick and help manifest your desired outcomes.

Intention: _____

Desired Outcome: _____

Notable Monthly Energies: _____

_____

Altar Aesthetics: _____

_____

_____

Altar Elements: _____

_____

Intentions

Utilize an intention to form the foundation of your manifestation, which means creating the desired outcome in accordance with your will. Intentions are the purpose or reason for why you are creating a spell or engaging in any magickal practice.

This may be for love, good fortune, or to banish something from your life. When starting spell work, focus on intentions connected to yourself only, not others.

Even good magick can take on a life of its own and be unexpected, often tripling in power and energy and coming back to you —good, bad, or in a twisted form. When the time is right, choose as many intentions and cast as many protection charms, wellness, success, good fortune, and hope for love or companionship as you can manifest each month.

Intentions are woven into spells—spells hold the energy and the intention, working by following the path of least resistance. Start slow and small rather than aiming for unstoppable tidal waves.

Intention Setting

This month, choose 1-4 intentions to focus on, whether for the entire month, lunar cycle, or one per week, depending on how much you practice.

Setting clear and focused intentions is crucial in your magickal practice. Narrowing your focus helps channel your energy more effectively. Whether for self-improvement, attracting positivity, or banishing negativity, these intentions guide your magickal work and keep you aligned with your goals.

Review and select your intentions this month. Consistency and clarity are key, allowing your intentions to manifest through dedicated practice, repetition, effort, and willpower.

Adventure	Authenticity	Balance
Calm	Career	Change
Comfort	Communication	Community
Culture	Divine wisdom	Education
Energy	Family	Freedom
Friends	Fun	Growth
Happiness	Health	Honesty
Honoring	Integrity	Knowledge
Peace	Relationships	Resilience
Respect	Security	Self
Success	Travel	Trust
Wealth	Will	Wisdom

Spell Casting

TRANSFORM AN INTENTION INTO A SPELL

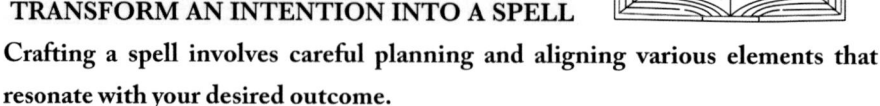

Crafting a spell involves careful planning and aligning various elements that resonate with your desired outcome.

Utilize spells to transform your intentions into reality. Use this template to plan and organize your spell work. Ensure each component supports and aligns with your intention, enhancing your magick with energy. By thoughtfully and mindfully selecting and arranging spell elements, you can amplify your magick and increase the effectiveness of your spell work. With focused intent and deliberate action, you will manifest your desires and achieve your goals.

Making Magick

When casting spells, consider which energies support your intention. Determine which correspondences, moon phases, planetary alignments, seasons, or times of day are best. Carefully selecting these elements enhances your spell's power and effectiveness.

Repetition Magick

Repetition Magick involves repeating your entire spell multiple times to strengthen the likelihood of achieving your desired outcome. This intensifies the energy and makes your spell more effective. **Never spell and tell before a spell has worked! It can muddle and redirect your focused energy, leading to negative results.**

Spell 1

Intention: _____

_____

Desired Outcome: _____

_____

_____

_____

Correspondences: _____

_____

_____

_____

_____

_____

_____

witchcraftspellsmagick.com

Spell 2

Intention: _____

_____

Desired Outcome: _____

_____

_____

_____

Correspondences: _____

_____

_____

_____

_____

_____

_____

Spell 3

Intention: _____

_____

Desired Outcome: _____

_____

_____

_____

Correspondences: _____

_____

_____

_____

_____

_____

_____

Spells are the manifestation of your will!

Spells are a powerful tool for you to work with to manifest your desires. By setting a clear intention and casting a spell during a ritual, you can transform energy and bend outcomes to your will. These incantations, also known as enchantments or bewitchery, take many forms—spoken, written, thought, chanted, or sung. Successful spell work requires an alchemical mix of components and a lot of practice and patience. With dedication and focus, you can utilize the power of spells to create your desired outcome.

Ritual Preparation

SACRED SPACE AND CIRCLE CASTING STEPS

Cast a circle before spell and ritual work, or anytime you want to invoke protection and create a sacred space. Here are some steps to guide you:

1. Preparation
Collect objects and prepare your space for ritual or spell work.

2. Purification
Cleanse the space and yourself.

3. Casting
Create a physical or psychic circle for protection and manifestation.

4. Invocation
Introduce the energies you intend to work with. Invocation: *"I/we graciously invoke you..."*

5. Intention
Use your tool to draw a pentagram and state your intention.

6. Ritual Practice
Meditation, trance work, psychic divination, dance, chanting, spell work...

7. Closing
Dance, sing, or share offerings.

8. Gratitude and Reflection
Give thanks to the divine, metaphysical, elemental, spirit, and mortal energies you have worked with.

Ritual 1

Intention: _____

Desired Outcome: _____

Notable Monthly Energies: _____

_____

Altar Aesthetics: _____

_____

Altar Elements: _____

_____

_____

witchcraftspellsmagick.com

Ritual 2

Intention: _____

Desired Outcome: _____

Notable Monthly Energies: _____

_____

Altar Aesthetics: _____

_____

Altar Elements: _____

_____

_____

1. Preparation, 2. Purification, 3. Casting, 4. Invocation,
5. Intention, 6. Ritual Practice, 7. Closing, 8. Gratitude and Reflection

Ritual 3

Intention: _____

Desired Outcome: _____

Notable Monthly Energies: _____

_____

Altar Aesthetics: _____

_____

Altar Elements: _____

_____

_____

June 2025

To do	NOTES

1st SUNDAY	To do

Magickal Focus: _____

Daily Affirmation: _____

_____

Reflective Journal Keywords: _____

_____

June 2025

2nd MONDAY	3rd TUESDAY
First Quarter Moon Magickal Focus: _____ Daily Affirmation: _____ _____ Reflective Journal Keywords: _____ _____	 Magickal Focus: _____ Daily Affirmation: _____ _____ Reflective Journal Keywords: _____ _____
4th WEDNESDAY	**5th THURSDAY**
     Magickal Focus: _____ Daily Affirmation: _____ _____ Reflective Journal Keywords: _____ _____	 Magickal Focus: _____ Daily Affirmation: _____ _____ Reflective Journal Keywords: _____ _____

6th FRIDAY	**7th SATURDAY**
Magickal Focus: _____ Daily Affirmation: _____ _____ Reflective Journal Keywords: _____ _____	Magickal Focus: _____ Daily Affirmation: _____ _____ Reflective Journal Keywords: _____ _____
8th SUNDAY	**To do**
Magickal Focus: _____ Daily Affirmation: _____ _____ Reflective Journal Keywords: _____ _____	

June 2025

9th MONDAY	10th TUESDAY
	Full Moon
Magickal Focus: _____	Magickal Focus: _____
Daily Affirmation: _____	Daily Affirmation: _____
Reflective Journal Keywords: _____	Reflective Journal Keywords: _____

11th WEDNESDAY	12th THURSDAY
Magickal Focus: _____	Magickal Focus: _____
Daily Affirmation: _____	Daily Affirmation: _____
Reflective Journal Keywords: _____	Reflective Journal Keywords: _____

witchcraftspellsmagick.com

13th FRIDAY

Magickal Focus: _____

Daily Affirmation: _____

_____

Reflective Journal Keywords: _____

_____

14th SATURDAY

Magickal Focus: _____

Daily Affirmation: _____

_____

Reflective Journal Keywords: _____

_____

15th SUNDAY

Magickal Focus: _____

Daily Affirmation: _____

_____

Reflective Journal Keywords: _____

_____

To do

June 2025

16th MONDAY

Magickal Focus: _____

Daily Affirmation: _____
_____

Reflective Journal Keywords: _____
_____

17th TUESDAY

Last Quarter Moon

Magickal Focus: _____

Daily Affirmation: _____
_____

Reflective Journal Keywords: _____
_____

18th WEDNESDAY

Magickal Focus: _____

Daily Affirmation: _____
_____

Reflective Journal Keywords: _____
_____

19th THURSDAY

Magickal Focus: _____

Daily Affirmation: _____
_____

Reflective Journal Keywords: _____
_____

20th FRIDAY

Magickal Focus: _____

Daily Affirmation: _____

_____

Reflective Journal Keywords: _____

_____

21st SATURDAY

Summer Solstice
Litha

Magickal Focus: _____

Daily Affirmation: _____

_____

Reflective Journal Keywords: _____

_____

22nd SUNDAY

Magickal Focus: _____

Daily Affirmation: _____

_____

Reflective Journal Keywords: _____

_____

To do

June 2025

23rd MONDAY	24th TUESDAY
      Magickal Focus: _____ Daily Affirmation: _____ _____ Reflective Journal Keywords: _____ _____	● *Dark Moon* Magickal Focus: _____ Daily Affirmation: _____ _____ Reflective Journal Keywords: _____ _____
25th WEDNESDAY	**26th THURSDAY**
      Magickal Focus: _____ Daily Affirmation: _____ _____ Reflective Journal Keywords: _____ _____	 Magickal Focus: _____ Daily Affirmation: _____ _____ Reflective Journal Keywords: _____ _____

27th FRIDAY	28th SATURDAY
Magickal Focus: _____	Magickal Focus: _____
Daily Affirmation: _____	Daily Affirmation: _____
Reflective Journal Keywords: _____	Reflective Journal Keywords: _____
29th SUNDAY	**To do**
Magickal Focus: _____	
Daily Affirmation: _____	
Reflective Journal Keywords: _____	

June 2025

30th MONDAY	NOTES
Magickal Focus:_____ Daily Affirmation:_____ Reflective Journal Keywords:_____	

NOTES	To do
Magickal Focus:_____ Daily Affirmation:_____ Reflective Journal Keywords:_____	

witchcraftspellsmagick.com

July 2025

Monday	Tuesday	Wednesday	Thursday	Friday
30	1	2 *First Quarter Moon*	3	4
7	8	9 *Full Moon in Capricorn*	10	11
14	15	16	17 *Last Quarter Moon*	18
21	22	23 *Dark Moon*	24	25
28	29	30	31	1
4	5	6	7	8

witchcraftspellsmagick.com

2025 Book of Shadows 209

Saturday	Sunday
5	6
12	13
19	20
26	27
2	3
9	10

This Month

Lunar Cycle Intention:

_____
_____

Most Important Events:

1. _____
2. _____
3. _____
4. _____
5. _____

To Do List:

○ _____
○ _____
○ _____
○ _____
○ _____
○ _____
○ _____

Notes & Thoughts:

July 2025

MOON ESBAT - Witches' Sabbat

The July Moon Esbat is observed on the 9th in the Northern Hemisphere and the 11th in the Southern Hemisphere, is a sacred celebration focused on connecting with the Triple Goddess.

A Moon Esbat can be any ritual or magickal work done during any moon phase, not just the full moon. These rituals provide an opportunity for you to attune to lunar energies and honor the phases of the moon. The Maiden represents the new moon, the Mother the full moon, and the Crone the waning moon. Esbats are ideal for your practice and connection between Sabbats.

During a full moon, emotions may be heightened, making it important to base decisions on clear, rational thinking rather than impulsive feelings. The full moon acts as nature's catalyst, awakening you from routine and bringing new perspectives.

The moon, embodying femininity, offers a chance for sharing, teaching, healing, and learning. Esbats carry a distinctively different energy compared to the Sabbats, contributing to a balanced and harmonious practice.

This Month's
RITUAL INSPIRATION
CRYSTAL GRID - Powerful Energies

Arrange your crystals on a geometric grid to manifest healing energies, prosperity, love, or courage during the July Moon Esbat.

RITUAL BATH - Clear Negative Energy

Indulge in a magickal ceremony of cleansing and revitalizing water. Add moon water, flower petals, and a few drops of essential oils to your bath.

MOTHER BLESSING - Honoring Mothers

The full moon is a time to celebrate our Divine Mother—the Moon—and honor all mothers. Recognize Mother Earth and our personal mothers for their nurturing and unconditional love. Write down thoughts, share, and create flower bouquets during a 'Mother Blessing' ritual.

witchcraftspellsmagick.com

Tarot Reading

Monthly Tarot readings offer you valuable guidance and insight for the month ahead. To start, shuffle your cards for at least 30-40 seconds while focusing on a specific question or area of your life that you would like guidance on.

When you're ready, lay down the top three cards to represent the past, present, and future. For further details on tarot, visit witchcraftspellsmagick.com

Past *Where you have been.*	**Current** *Where you are now.*	**Future** *Where you are going next.*

Deck: _____ **Date:** _____

Card 1 - Past: _____

_____

_____

Card 2 - Current: _____

_____

_____

Card 3 - Future: _____

_____

_____

July Magickal Correspondences

July brings the peak of summer's warmth and vitality, a time when nature is in full bloom and the energies of the sun are at their most potent.

The days are long and bright, fostering a sense of joy, abundance, and exuberant growth. This month is ideal for focusing on magickal practices that celebrate the power of the sun, personal strength, and the fulfillment of goals.

Animals - Bat, Bee, Butterfly, Dove, Frog, Owl, Rabbit, Wolf
Aromatics - Jasmine, Lilac, Rose, Sage, Sandalwood, Sweetgrass
Colors - Pale Blue, Purple, Silver, White
Crystals - Clear Quartz, Emerald, Jade, Malachite, Moonstone
Flowers - Daisy, Hawthorn, Night-Blooming Jasmine, Peony, Rose, White Roses
Fruit - Apple, Cherry, Strawberry, Blueberry, Lemon, Orange
Herbs - Basil, Elderflower, Mint, Mugwort, Thyme
Spice - Cinnamon, Clove, Ginger
Trees - Hawthorn, Maple, Oak, Rowan, Willow

ALTAR CHECKLIST
Moon Esbat
Altar Setup Basics - Start with the Elements:
Earth: Pentacle | Water: Chalice
Air: Incense or Diffuser | Fire: Candle

Additional Ideas:
- Gratitude list
- Moon cookies
- Triple Moon Goddess statue
- Moon altar cloth | Moon-shaped plate
- Tarot | Oracle cards
- Bowl of salt
- Runes
- Rose petals | Shells
- Silver sacred objects

Notes & Thoughts:

witchcraftspellsmagick.com

[Sketch Your Altar Setup]

Altar Planning

Creating a monthly altar helps you align with the cycles of nature and set focused intentions for your magickal practices.

Use this template to plan and organize your altar setup, ensuring that each element supports your intention and enhances your connection to the energies of the month. Thoughtful planning and intentional arrangement of your altar will amplify your magick and help manifest your desired outcomes.

Intention: _____

Desired Outcome: _____

Notable Monthly Energies: _____

_____

Altar Aesthetics: _____

_____

_____

Altar Elements: _____

_____

Intentions

Utilize an intention to form the foundation of your manifestation, which means creating the desired outcome in accordance with your will. Intentions are the purpose or reason for why you are creating a spell or engaging in any magickal practice.

This may be for love, good fortune, or to banish something from your life. When starting spell work, focus on intentions connected to yourself only, not others.

Even good magick can take on a life of its own and be unexpected, often tripling in power and energy and coming back to you —good, bad, or in a twisted form. When the time is right, choose as many intentions and cast as many protection charms, wellness, success, good fortune, and hope for love or companionship as you can manifest each month.

Intentions are woven into spells—spells hold the energy and the intention, working by following the path of least resistance. Start slow and small rather than aiming for unstoppable tidal waves.

Intention Setting

This month, choose 1-4 intentions to focus on, whether for the entire month, lunar cycle, or one per week, depending on how much you practice.

Setting clear and focused intentions is crucial in your magickal practice. Narrowing your focus helps channel your energy more effectively. Whether for self-improvement, attracting positivity, or banishing negativity, these intentions guide your magickal work and keep you aligned with your goals.

Review and select your intentions this month. Consistency and clarity are key, allowing your intentions to manifest through dedicated practice, repetition, effort, and willpower.

Adventure	Authenticity	Balance
Calm	Career	Change
Comfort	Communication	Community
Culture	Divine wisdom	Education
Energy	Family	Freedom
Friends	Fun	Growth
Happiness	Health	Honesty
Honoring	Integrity	Knowledge
Peace	Relationships	Resilience
Respect	Security	Self
Success	Travel	Trust
Wealth	Will	Wisdom

Spell Casting

TRANSFORM AN INTENTION INTO A SPELL

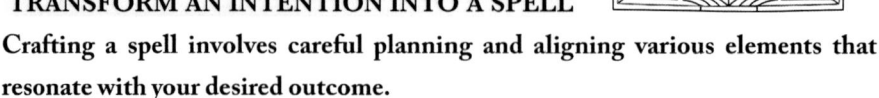

Crafting a spell involves careful planning and aligning various elements that resonate with your desired outcome.

    Utilize spells to transform your intentions into reality. Use this template to plan and organize your spell work. Ensure each component supports and aligns with your intention, enhancing your magick with energy. By thoughtfully and mindfully selecting and arranging spell elements, you can amplify your magick and increase the effectiveness of your spell work. With focused intent and deliberate action, you will manifest your desires and achieve your goals.

Making Magick

When casting spells, consider which energies support your intention. Determine which correspondences, moon phases, planetary alignments, seasons, or times of day are best. Carefully selecting these elements enhances your spell's power and effectiveness.

Repetition Magick

Repetition Magick involves repeating your entire spell multiple times to strengthen the likelihood of achieving your desired outcome. This intensifies the energy and makes your spell more effective.

Never spell and tell before a spell has worked! It can muddle and redirect your focused energy, leading to negative results.

Spell 1

Intention: _____

_____

Desired Outcome: _____

_____

_____

_____

Correspondences: _____

_____

_____

_____

_____

_____

_____

_____

witchcraftspellsmagick.com

Spell 2

Intention: _____

_____

Desired Outcome: _____

_____

_____

Correspondences: _____

_____

_____

_____

_____

_____

Spell 3

Intention: _____

_____

Desired Outcome: _____

_____

_____

Correspondences: _____

_____

_____

_____

_____

_____

Spells are the manifestation of your will!

Spells are a powerful tool for you to work with to manifest your desires. By setting a clear intention and casting a spell during a ritual, you can transform energy and bend outcomes to your will. These incantations, also known as enchantments or bewitchery, take many forms—spoken, written, thought, chanted, or sung. Successful spell work requires an alchemical mix of components and a lot of practice and patience. With dedication and focus, you can utilize the power of spells to create your desired outcome.

Ritual Preparation

SACRED SPACE AND CIRCLE CASTING STEPS

Cast a circle before spell and ritual work, or anytime you want to invoke protection and create a sacred space. Here are some steps to guide you:

1. Preparation
Collect objects and prepare your space for ritual or spell work.

2. Purification
Cleanse the space and yourself.

3. Casting
Create a physical or psychic circle for protection and manifestation.

4. Invocation
Introduce the energies you intend to work with. Invocation: *"I/we graciously invoke you..."*

5. Intention
Use your tool to draw a pentagram and state your intention.

6. Ritual Practice
Meditation, trance work, psychic divination, dance, chanting, spell work...

7. Closing
Dance, sing, or share offerings.

8. Gratitude and Reflection
Give thanks to the divine, metaphysical, elemental, spirit, and mortal energies you have worked with.

Ritual 1

Intention: _____

Desired Outcome: _____

Notable Monthly Energies: _____

_____

Altar Aesthetics: _____

_____

Altar Elements: _____

_____

_____

Ritual 2

Intention: _____

Desired Outcome: _____

Notable Monthly Energies: _____
_____

Altar Aesthetics: _____
_____

Altar Elements: _____
_____
_____

> 1. Preparation, 2. Purification, 3. Casting, 4. Invocation,
> 5. Intention, 6. Ritual Practice, 7. Closing, 8. Gratitude and Reflection

Ritual 3

Intention: _____

Desired Outcome: _____

Notable Monthly Energies: _____
_____

Altar Aesthetics: _____
_____

Altar Elements: _____
_____
_____

July 2025

To do	1st TUESDAY
	Magickal Focus: _____ Daily Affirmation: _____ _____ Reflective Journal Keywords: _____ _____
2nd WEDNESDAY	**3rd THURSDAY**
First Quarter Moon Magickal Focus: _____ Daily Affirmation: _____ _____ Reflective Journal Keywords: _____ _____	Magickal Focus: _____ Daily Affirmation: _____ _____ Reflective Journal Keywords: _____ _____

witchcraftspellsmagick.com

2025 Book of Shadows

4th FRIDAY

Magickal Focus: _____

Daily Affirmation: _____

_____

Reflective Journal Keywords: _____

_____

5th SATURDAY

Magickal Focus: _____

Daily Affirmation: _____

_____

Reflective Journal Keywords: _____

_____

6th SUNDAY

Magickal Focus: _____

Daily Affirmation: _____

_____

Reflective Journal Keywords: _____

_____

To do

July 2025

7th MONDAY	**8th TUESDAY**
Magickal Focus: _____ Daily Affirmation: _____ _____ Reflective Journal Keywords: _____ _____	Magickal Focus: _____ Daily Affirmation: _____ _____ Reflective Journal Keywords: _____ _____
9th WEDNESDAY	**10th THURSDAY**
Full Moon Magickal Focus: _____ Daily Affirmation: _____ _____ Reflective Journal Keywords: _____ _____	Magickal Focus: _____ Daily Affirmation: _____ _____ Reflective Journal Keywords: _____ _____

witchcraftspellsmagick.com

11th FRIDAY

Magickal Focus: _____

Daily Affirmation: _____

_____

Reflective Journal Keywords: _____

_____

12th SATURDAY

Magickal Focus: _____

Daily Affirmation: _____

_____

Reflective Journal Keywords: _____

_____

13th SUNDAY

Magickal Focus: _____

Daily Affirmation: _____

_____

Reflective Journal Keywords: _____

_____

To do

July 2025

14th MONDAY	15th TUESDAY
Magickal Focus: _____ Daily Affirmation: _____ _____ Reflective Journal Keywords: _____ _____	Magickal Focus: _____ Daily Affirmation: _____ _____ Reflective Journal Keywords: _____ _____
16th WEDNESDAY	**17th THURSDAY** *Last Quarter Moon*
Magickal Focus: _____ Daily Affirmation: _____ _____ Reflective Journal Keywords: _____ _____	Magickal Focus: _____ Daily Affirmation: _____ _____ Reflective Journal Keywords: _____ _____

18th FRIDAY	19th SATURDAY
Magickal Focus: _____ Daily Affirmation: _____ _____ Reflective Journal Keywords: _____ _____	Magickal Focus: _____ Daily Affirmation: _____ _____ Reflective Journal Keywords: _____ _____
20th SUNDAY	**To do**
Magickal Focus: _____ Daily Affirmation: _____ _____ Reflective Journal Keywords: _____ _____	

July 2025

21st MONDAY	22nd TUESDAY
Magickal Focus: _____ Daily Affirmation: _____ _____ Reflective Journal Keywords: _____ _____	Magickal Focus: _____ Daily Affirmation: _____ _____ Reflective Journal Keywords: _____ _____

23rd WEDNESDAY	24th THURSDAY
● *Dark Moon* Magickal Focus: _____ Daily Affirmation: _____ _____ Reflective Journal Keywords: _____ _____	Magickal Focus: _____ Daily Affirmation: _____ _____ Reflective Journal Keywords: _____ _____

witchcraftspellsmagick.com

25th FRIDAY

Magickal Focus: _____

Daily Affirmation: _____

_____

Reflective Journal Keywords: _____

_____

26th SATURDAY

Magickal Focus: _____

Daily Affirmation: _____

_____

Reflective Journal Keywords: _____

_____

27th SUNDAY

Magickal Focus: _____

Daily Affirmation: _____

_____

Reflective Journal Keywords: _____

_____

To do

July 2025

28th MONDAY

Magickal Focus: _____

Daily Affirmation: _____
_____

Reflective Journal Keywords: _____
_____

29th TUESDAY

Magickal Focus: _____

Daily Affirmation: _____
_____

Reflective Journal Keywords: _____
_____

30th WEDNESDAY

Magickal Focus: _____

Daily Affirmation: _____
_____

Reflective Journal Keywords: _____
_____

31st THURSDAY

Magickal Focus: _____

Daily Affirmation: _____
_____

Reflective Journal Keywords: _____
_____

witchcraftspellsmagick.com

August 2025

Monday	Tuesday	Wednesday	Thursday	Friday
28	29	30	31	1 *Lughnasadh* *First Quarter Moon*
4	5	6	7	8
11	12	13	14	15 *Last Quarter Moon*
18	19	20	21	22 *Dark Moon*
25	26	27	28	29
1	2	3	4	5

witchcraftspellsmagick.com

2025 Book of Shadows

Saturday	Sunday
2	3
9 *Full Moon in Aquarius*	10
16	17
23	24
30 *First Quarter Moon*	31
6	7

This Month

Lunar Cycle Intention:
_____
_____

Most Important Events:
1. _____
2. _____
3. _____
4. _____
5. _____

To Do List:
○ _____
○ _____
○ _____
○ _____
○ _____
○ _____
○ _____

Notes & Thoughts:

August 2025

LUGHNASADH - Greater Witches' Sabbat

Lughnasadh or Lammas is observed on the 1st of August in the Northern Hemisphere and the 1st of February in the Southern Hemisphere, is a sacred celebration with deep Celtic origins.

This festival, also known as Lughnasadh (pronounced loo'nass'ah), honors the Irish God Lugh and marks the first day of the harvest season.

The Anglo-Saxons later celebrated this festival as Half-mass, Loaf-mass, or Lammas. Lughnasadh signifies a time to honor the Gods and nature, hoping for a prosperous harvest. The harvest continues through three celebrations: Lughnasadh, Mabon, and Samhain, when the final harvest stores are put away for the winter months.

Modern witches celebrate Lughnasadh with gratitude for all earthly and physical sustenance. As we gather to honor this Sabbat, we embrace the bounty of the first harvest, reflecting on the cycle of growth and the promise of abundance that Lughnasadh brings.

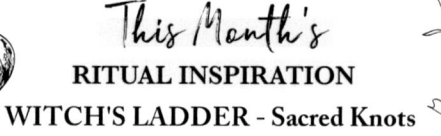

This Month's RITUAL INSPIRATION
WITCH'S LADDER - Sacred Knots

Create a Witch's Ladder with intentional knots, feathers, and beads for protection and good fortune.

OFFERING - Bake Bread

Bake bread as an altar offering after ritual work. This symbolizes abundance and gratitude, connecting you with the earth's bountiful gifts during Lughnasadh.

CORN DOLL - Protective Magickal Charms

1. Wash and dry corn husks, lay an even number on top of each other.
2. Tie one end together leaving an inch (2.5cm).
3. Pull the long ends over the tied ends to form the head.
4. Lay what will be the arms through horizontally, tie the ends to form the hands.
5. Tie the waist and divide the remaining in half to form the legs.
6. Clothe your doll in cloth and decorate as you choose.

Tarot Reading

Monthly Tarot readings offer you valuable guidance and insight for the month ahead. To start, shuffle your cards for at least 30-40 seconds while focusing on a specific question or area of your life that you would like guidance on.

When you're ready, lay down the top three cards to represent the past, present, and future. For further details on tarot, visit witchcraftspellsmagick.com

Past	**Current**	**Future**
Where you have been.	*Where you are now.*	*Where you are going next.*

Deck: _____ Date: _____

Card 1 - Past: _____

_____

_____

Card 2 - Current: _____

_____

_____

Card 3 - Future: _____

_____

_____

August Magickal Correspondences

During August, the season transitions into the time of the first harvest, a period of gratitude and transformation.

Lughnasadh, celebrated at the start of the month, marks the beginning of the reaping season, symbolizing abundance and the fruits of our labor. This is a time to honor the earth's bounty and reflect on the balance between giving and receiving.

Animals - Bees, Butterfly, Rabbit, Phoenix, Horse, Lambs
Colors - Pastels, Gold, White, Green, Yellow
Crystals - Aquamarine, Jade, Agate, Bloodstone, Ruby, Rose Quartz
Flowers - Lilac, Narcissus, Rose, Peonies, Tulips, Violets
Fruit - Lemon, Orange, Lime, Grapefruit, Apple, Strawberry, Cherry
Herbs - Lemon Verbena, Rosemary, Mint, Basil, Thyme
Aromatics - Lavender, Red Cedar, Geranium, Vetiver, Sandalwood, Chamomile
Spices - Clove, Cinnamon, Nutmeg, Ginger, Cardamom
Trees - Pine, Alder, Hawthorn, Birch, Willow

ALTAR CHECKLIST
Gratitude, Humility + for Harvest Blessings
Altar Setup Basics - Start with the Elements:
Earth: Pentacle | Water: Chalice
Air: Incense or Diffuser | Fire: Candle

Additional Ideas:
- Lugh statue | Sun symbol
- Corn doll | Corn husk | Jar of kernels
- Baked bread | Wheat
- Harvest veggies and grains
- Gratitude cards | Pebbles (for humility)
- Bowl of seeds | Sunflowers
- Witches Ladder
- Seasonal herbs | Symbols of growth
- Solar lights or lanterns

Notes & Thoughts:

witchcraftspellsmagick.com

Sketch Your Altar Setup

Altar Planning

Creating a monthly altar helps you align with the cycles of nature and set focused intentions for your magickal practices.

Use this template to plan and organize your altar setup, ensuring that each element supports your intention and enhances your connection to the energies of the month. Thoughtful planning and intentional arrangement of your altar will amplify your magick and help manifest your desired outcomes.

Intention: _____

Desired Outcome: _____

Notable Monthly Energies: _____
_____

Altar Aesthetics: _____
_____
_____

Altar Elements: _____
_____

Intentions

Utilize an intention to form the foundation of your manifestation, which means creating the desired outcome in accordance with your will. Intentions are the purpose or reason for why you are creating a spell or engaging in any magickal practice.

This may be for love, good fortune, or to banish something from your life. When starting spell work, focus on intentions connected to yourself only, not others.

Even good magick can take on a life of its own and be unexpected, often tripling in power and energy and coming back to you —good, bad, or in a twisted form. When the time is right, choose as many intentions and cast as many protection charms, wellness, success, good fortune, and hope for love or companionship as you can manifest each month.

Intentions are woven into spells—spells hold the energy and the intention, working by following the path of least resistance. Start slow and small rather than aiming for unstoppable tidal waves.

Intention Setting

This month, choose 1-4 intentions to focus on, whether for the entire month, lunar cycle, or one per week, depending on how much you practice.

Setting clear and focused intentions is crucial in your magickal practice. Narrowing your focus helps channel your energy more effectively. Whether for self-improvement, attracting positivity, or banishing negativity, these intentions guide your magickal work and keep you aligned with your goals.

Review and select your intentions this month. Consistency and clarity are key, allowing your intentions to manifest through dedicated practice, repetition, effort, and willpower.

Adventure	Authenticity	Balance
Calm	Career	Change
Comfort	Communication	Community
Culture	Divine wisdom	Education
Energy	Family	Freedom
Friends	Fun	Growth
Happiness	Health	Honesty
Honoring	Integrity	Knowledge
Peace	Relationships	Resilience
Respect	Security	Self
Success	Travel	Trust
Wealth	Will	Wisdom

Spell Casting

TRANSFORM AN INTENTION INTO A SPELL

Crafting a spell involves careful planning and aligning various elements that resonate with your desired outcome.

Utilize spells to transform your intentions into reality. Use this template to plan and organize your spell work. Ensure each component supports and aligns with your intention, enhancing your magick with energy. By thoughtfully and mindfully selecting and arranging spell elements, you can amplify your magick and increase the effectiveness of your spell work. With focused intent and deliberate action, you will manifest your desires and achieve your goals.

Making Magick

When casting spells, consider which energies support your intention. Determine which correspondences, moon phases, planetary alignments, seasons, or times of day are best. Carefully selecting these elements enhances your spell's power and effectiveness.

Repetition Magick

Repetition Magick involves repeating your entire spell multiple times to strengthen the likelihood of achieving your desired outcome. This intensifies the energy and makes your spell more effective.

Never spell and tell before a spell has worked! It can muddle and redirect your focused energy, leading to negative results.

Spell 1

Intention: _____

_____

Desired Outcome: _____

_____

_____

_____

Correspondences: _____

_____

_____

_____

_____

_____

_____

_____

witchcraftspellsmagick.com

Spell 2

Intention: _____

_____

Desired Outcome: _____

_____

_____

_____

Correspondences: _____

_____

_____

_____

_____

_____

_____

Spell 3

Intention: _____

_____

Desired Outcome: _____

_____

_____

_____

Correspondences: _____

_____

_____

_____

_____

_____

_____

Spells are the manifestation of your will!

Spells are a powerful tool for you to work with to manifest your desires. By setting a clear intention and casting a spell during a ritual, you can transform energy and bend outcomes to your will. These incantations, also known as enchantments or bewitchery, take many forms—spoken, written, thought, chanted, or sung. Successful spell work requires an alchemical mix of components and a lot of practice and patience. With dedication and focus, you can utilize the power of spells to create your desired outcome.

Ritual Preparation

SACRED SPACE AND CIRCLE CASTING STEPS

Cast a circle before spell and ritual work, or anytime you want to invoke protection and create a sacred space. Here are some steps to guide you:

1. Preparation
Collect objects and prepare your space for ritual or spell work.

2. Purification
Cleanse the space and yourself.

3. Casting
Create a physical or psychic circle for protection and manifestation.

4. Invocation
Introduce the energies you intend to work with. Invocation: *"I/we graciously invoke you..."*

5. Intention
Use your tool to draw a pentagram and state your intention.

6. Ritual Practice
Meditation, trance work, psychic divination, dance, chanting, spell work...

7. Closing
Dance, sing, or share offerings.

8. Gratitude and Reflection
Give thanks to the divine, metaphysical, elemental, spirit, and mortal energies you have worked with.

Ritual 1

Intention: _____

Desired Outcome: _____

Notable Monthly Energies: _____

_____

Altar Aesthetics: _____

_____

Altar Elements: _____

_____

_____

Ritual 2

Intention: _____

Desired Outcome: _____

Notable Monthly Energies: _____

_____

Altar Aesthetics: _____

_____

Altar Elements: _____

_____

_____

---

1. Preparation, 2. Purification, 3. Casting, 4. Invocation,
5. Intention, 6. Ritual Practice, 7. Closing, 8. Gratitude and Reflection

---

Ritual 3

Intention: _____

Desired Outcome: _____

Notable Monthly Energies: _____

_____

Altar Aesthetics: _____

_____

Altar Elements: _____

_____

_____

August 2025

1st FRIDAY	2nd SATURDAY
Lughnasadh *First Quarter Moon* Magickal Focus: _____ Daily Affirmation: _____ _____ Reflective Journal Keywords: _____ _____	Magickal Focus: _____ Daily Affirmation: _____ _____ Reflective Journal Keywords: _____ _____
3rd SUNDAY	**To do**
    Magickal Focus: _____ Daily Affirmation: _____ _____ Reflective Journal Keywords: _____ _____	

August 2025

4th MONDAY	5th TUESDAY
Magickal Focus: _____ Daily Affirmation: _____ _____ Reflective Journal Keywords: _____ _____	Magickal Focus: _____ Daily Affirmation: _____ _____ Reflective Journal Keywords: _____ _____
6th WEDNESDAY	7th THURSDAY
Magickal Focus: _____ Daily Affirmation: _____ _____ Reflective Journal Keywords: _____ _____	Magickal Focus: _____ Daily Affirmation: _____ _____ Reflective Journal Keywords: _____ _____

8th FRIDAY	9th SATURDAY
	Full Moon
Magickal Focus: _____	Magickal Focus: _____
Daily Affirmation: _____	Daily Affirmation: _____
Reflective Journal Keywords: _____	Reflective Journal Keywords: _____
10th SUNDAY	**To do**
Magickal Focus: _____	
Daily Affirmation: _____	
Reflective Journal Keywords: _____	

August 2025

11th MONDAY	12th TUESDAY
Magickal Focus: _____ Daily Affirmation: _____ _____ Reflective Journal Keywords: _____ _____	Magickal Focus: _____ Daily Affirmation: _____ _____ Reflective Journal Keywords: _____ _____
13th WEDNESDAY	**14th THURSDAY**
Magickal Focus: _____ Daily Affirmation: _____ _____ Reflective Journal Keywords: _____ _____	Magickal Focus: _____ Daily Affirmation: _____ _____ Reflective Journal Keywords: _____ _____

witchcraftspellsmagick.com

15th FRIDAY

Last Quarter Moon

Magickal Focus: _____

Daily Affirmation: _____

_____

Reflective Journal Keywords: _____

_____

16th SATURDAY

Magickal Focus: _____

Daily Affirmation: _____

_____

Reflective Journal Keywords: _____

_____

17th SUNDAY

Magickal Focus: _____

Daily Affirmation: _____

_____

Reflective Journal Keywords: _____

_____

To do

August 2025

18th MONDAY	19th TUESDAY
Magickal Focus: _____ Daily Affirmation: _____ _____ Reflective Journal Keywords: _____ _____	Magickal Focus: _____ Daily Affirmation: _____ _____ Reflective Journal Keywords: _____ _____
20th WEDNESDAY	**21st THURSDAY**
Magickal Focus: _____ Daily Affirmation: _____ _____ Reflective Journal Keywords: _____ _____	Magickal Focus: _____ Daily Affirmation: _____ _____ Reflective Journal Keywords: _____ _____

witchcraftspellsmagick.com

22nd FRIDAY

●
Dark Moon

Magickal Focus: _____

Daily Affirmation: _____
_____

Reflective Journal Keywords: _____
_____

23rd SATURDAY

Magickal Focus: _____

Daily Affirmation: _____
_____

Reflective Journal Keywords: _____
_____

24th SUNDAY

Magickal Focus: _____

Daily Affirmation: _____
_____

Reflective Journal Keywords: _____
_____

To do

August 2025

25th MONDAY

Magickal Focus: _____

Daily Affirmation: _____
_____

Reflective Journal Keywords: _____
_____

26th TUESDAY

Magickal Focus: _____

Daily Affirmation: _____
_____

Reflective Journal Keywords: _____
_____

27th WEDNESDAY

Magickal Focus: _____

Daily Affirmation: _____
_____

Reflective Journal Keywords: _____
_____

28th THURSDAY

Magickal Focus: _____

Daily Affirmation: _____
_____

Reflective Journal Keywords: _____
_____

witchcraftspellsmagick.com

29th FRIDAY	**30th SATURDAY**
	First Quarter Moon
Magickal Focus: _____	Magickal Focus: _____
Daily Affirmation: _____	Daily Affirmation: _____
Reflective Journal Keywords: _____	Reflective Journal Keywords: _____
31st SUNDAY	**To do**
Magickal Focus: _____	
Daily Affirmation: _____	
Reflective Journal Keywords: _____	

September 2025

Monday	Tuesday	Wednesday	Thursday	Friday
25	26	27	28	29
1	2	3	4	5
8	9	10	11	12
15	16	17	18	19
22 *Autumn Equinox Mabon*	23	24	25	26
29	30	1	2	3

witchcraftspellsmagick.com

2025 Book of Shadows 253

Saturday	Sunday
30	31
6 *Full Moon in Pisces*	7
13 *Last Quarter Moon*	14
20 *Dark Moon*	21
27	28 *First Quarter Moon*
4	5

This Month

Lunar Cycle Intention:

_____

_____

Most Important Events:

1. _____
2. _____
3. _____
4. _____
5. _____

To Do List:

○ _____
○ _____
○ _____
○ _____
○ _____
○ _____
○ _____

Notes & Thoughts:

September 2025

Autumn Equinox | MABON - Lesser Witches' Sabbat
Mabon is observed on the 22nd of September in the Northern Hemisphere and the 20th of March in the Southern Hemisphere. It is a sacred celebration of ancient lore and rich symbolism.

This festival marks the Autumn Equinox, a time when day and night are equal, symbolizing balance and reflection. Mabon signifies the second harvest, a time to give thanks for the earth's abundance and prepare for winter. This period honors the God and Goddess, celebrating the fruits of our labor and the blessings of the harvest season. Named after the Welsh God Mabon, a figure of strength and maturity, the festival reflects his story of being kidnapped and hidden in darkness, symbolizing the journey into the dark half of the year.

As nature transforms, Mabon heralds a time of balance and transition, where summer's vibrant energy gives way to autumn's introspective mood. As we gather to honor this Sabbat, we do so with hearts filled with gratitude and minds attuned to nature's cycles, embracing life's perpetual rhythm and the renewal that Mabon brings.

This Month's
RITUAL INSPIRATION
BESOM - Home Cleanse

A besom is a witch's broom used to shift energy. Walk your house, brushing your besom above the floor to remove negative or stagnant energies and replace them with refreshed, cleansed energy during Mabon.

DONATIONS - Act of Kindness

Offer unwanted, good condition clothes and objects to others.
This aligns with Mabon's spirit of sharing abundance and generosity.

SALT OFFERING - Home Blessing

Mix 2 tablespoons of rock salt with 3 crushed pinches of rosemary. Sprinkle or place in bowls around your home, focusing on windows and door corners, to bless and protect your space during Mabon.

witchcraftspellsmagick.com

Tarot Reading

Monthly Tarot readings offer you valuable guidance and insight for the month ahead. To start, shuffle your cards for at least 30-40 seconds while focusing on a specific question or area of your life that you would like guidance on.

When you're ready, lay down the top three cards to represent the past, present, and future. For further details on tarot, visit witchcraftspellsmagick.com

Past
Where you have been.

Current
Where you are now.

Future
Where you are going next.

Deck: _____ **Date:** _____

Card 1 - Past: _____

_____

_____

Card 2 - Current: _____

_____

_____

Card 3 - Future: _____

_____

_____

September Magickal Correspondences

During September, the season transitions to autumn, a time for home blessing, balance and transformation.

Mabon, the Autumn Equinox, marks a moment of equal day and night, symbolizing harmony and gratitude for the harvest. This is a time to celebrate abundance, reflect on personal growth, and prepare for the coming winter.

Animals - Blackbird, Fox, Owl, Rabbit, Stag, Wolf
Colours - Black, Brown, Green, Orange, Red, Yellow
Crystals - Amber, Citrine, Clear quartz, Garnet, Jet, Tiger's eye, Yellow topaz
Flowers - Daisy, Dandelion, Marigold, Rose, Sunflower, Thistle
Fruits + Vegetables - Apple, Carrot, Grape, Pomegranate, Pumpkin
Herbs - Basil, Mint, Rosemary, Rosehip, Rue, Saffron, Thyme
Aromatics - Cinnamon, Frankincense, Lavender, Myrrh, Sage, Sandalwood
Spices - Cinnamon, Clove, Nutmeg, Star anise
Trees - Birch, Cedar, Oak, Pine, Willow

ALTAR CHECKLIST
Home Blessing
Altar Setup Basics - Start with the Elements:
Earth: Pentacle | Water: Chalice
Air: Incense or Diffuser | Fire: Candle

Additional Ideas:
- Gratitude list
- Basket with Autumn fruit
- Autumn leaves or flowers | Wicker basket
- Salt | Altar bowls
- Besom
- Corn | Root Vegetables
- Fresh bread | Grains | Seeds
- Scales (symbol of balance)
- Solar lights or bright-colored candles

Notes & Thoughts:

witchcraftspellsmagick.com

[Sketch Your Altar Setup]

Altar Planning

Creating a monthly altar helps you align with the cycles of nature and set focused intentions for your magickal practices.

Use this template to plan and organize your altar setup, ensuring that each element supports your intention and enhances your connection to the energies of the month. Thoughtful planning and intentional arrangement of your altar will amplify your magick and help manifest your desired outcomes.

Intention: _____

Desired Outcome: _____

Notable Monthly Energies: _____

_____

Altar Aesthetics: _____

_____

_____

Altar Elements: _____

_____

Intentions

Utilize an intention to form the foundation of your manifestation, which means creating the desired outcome in accordance with your will. Intentions are the purpose or reason for why you are creating a spell or engaging in any magickal practice.

This may be for love, good fortune, or to banish something from your life. When starting spell work, focus on intentions connected to yourself only, not others.

Even good magick can take on a life of its own and be unexpected, often tripling in power and energy and coming back to you—good, bad, or in a twisted form. When the time is right, choose as many intentions and cast as many protection charms, wellness, success, good fortune, and hope for love or companionship as you can manifest each month.

Intentions are woven into spells—spells hold the energy and the intention, working by following the path of least resistance. Start slow and small rather than aiming for unstoppable tidal waves.

Intention Setting

This month, choose 1-4 intentions to focus on, whether for the entire month, lunar cycle, or one per week, depending on how much you practice.

Setting clear and focused intentions is crucial in your magickal practice. Narrowing your focus helps channel your energy more effectively. Whether for self-improvement, attracting positivity, or banishing negativity, these intentions guide your magickal work and keep you aligned with your goals.

Review and select your intentions this month. Consistency and clarity are key, allowing your intentions to manifest through dedicated practice, repetition, effort, and willpower.

Adventure	Authenticity	Balance
Calm	Career	Change
Comfort	Communication	Community
Culture	Divine wisdom	Education
Energy	Family	Freedom
Friends	Fun	Growth
Happiness	Health	Honesty
Honoring	Integrity	Knowledge
Peace	Relationships	Resilience
Respect	Security	Self
Success	Travel	Trust
Wealth	Will	Wisdom

Spell Casting

TRANSFORM AN INTENTION INTO A SPELL

Crafting a spell involves careful planning and aligning various elements that resonate with your desired outcome.

Utilize spells to transform your intentions into reality. Use this template to plan and organize your spell work. Ensure each component supports and aligns with your intention, enhancing your magick with energy. By thoughtfully and mindfully selecting and arranging spell elements, you can amplify your magick and increase the effectiveness of your spell work. With focused intent and deliberate action, you will manifest your desires and achieve your goals.

Making Magick

When casting spells, consider which energies support your intention. Determine which correspondences, moon phases, planetary alignments, seasons, or times of day are best. Carefully selecting these elements enhances your spell's power and effectiveness.

Repetition Magick

Repetition Magick involves repeating your entire spell multiple times to strengthen the likelihood of achieving your desired outcome. This intensifies the energy and makes your spell more effective.

Never spell and tell before a spell has worked! It can muddle and redirect your focused energy, leading to negative results.

Spell 1

Intention: _____

_____

Desired Outcome: _____

_____

_____

_____

Correspondences: _____

_____

_____

_____

_____

_____

_____

witchcraftspellsmagick.com

Spell 2

Intention: _____

_____

Desired Outcome: _____

_____

_____

_____

Correspondences: _____

_____

_____

_____

_____

_____

_____

Spell 3

Intention: _____

_____

Desired Outcome: _____

_____

_____

_____

Correspondences: _____

_____

_____

_____

_____

_____

_____

Spells are the manifestation of your will!

Spells are a powerful tool for you to work with to manifest your desires. By setting a clear intention and casting a spell during a ritual, you can transform energy and bend outcomes to your will. These incantations, also known as enchantments or bewitchery, take many forms—spoken, written, thought, chanted, or sung. Successful spell work requires an alchemical mix of components and a lot of practice and patience. With dedication and focus, you can utilize the power of spells to create your desired outcome.

Ritual Preparation

SACRED SPACE AND CIRCLE CASTING STEPS

Cast a circle before spell and ritual work, or anytime you want to invoke protection and create a sacred space. Here are some steps to guide you:

1. Preparation
Collect objects and prepare your space for ritual or spell work.

2. Purification
Cleanse the space and yourself.

3. Casting
Create a physical or psychic circle for protection and manifestation.

4. Invocation
Introduce the energies you intend to work with. Invocation: *"I/we graciously invoke you..."*

5. Intention
Use your tool to draw a pentagram and state your intention.

6. Ritual Practice
Meditation, trance work, psychic divination, dance, chanting, spell work...

7. Closing
Dance, sing, or share offerings.

8. Gratitude and Reflection
Give thanks to the divine, metaphysical, elemental, spirit, and mortal energies you have worked with.

Ritual 1

Intention: _____

Desired Outcome: _____

Notable Monthly Energies: _____

_____

Altar Aesthetics: _____

_____

Altar Elements: _____

_____

_____

witchcraftspellsmagick.com

Ritual 2

Intention: _____

Desired Outcome: _____

Notable Monthly Energies: _____
_____

Altar Aesthetics: _____
_____

Altar Elements: _____
_____
_____

1. Preparation, 2. Purification, 3. Casting, 4. Invocation,
5. Intention, 6. Ritual Practice, 7. Closing, 8. Gratitude and Reflection

Ritual 3

Intention: _____

Desired Outcome: _____

Notable Monthly Energies: _____
_____

Altar Aesthetics: _____
_____

Altar Elements: _____
_____
_____

September 2025

1st MONDAY	2nd TUESDAY
Magickal Focus: _____ Daily Affirmation: _____ Reflective Journal Keywords: _____	Magickal Focus: _____ Daily Affirmation: _____ Reflective Journal Keywords: _____
3rd WEDNESDAY	**4th THURSDAY**
Magickal Focus: _____ Daily Affirmation: _____ Reflective Journal Keywords: _____	Magickal Focus: _____ Daily Affirmation: _____ Reflective Journal Keywords: _____

witchcraftspellsmagick.com

5th FRIDAY

Magickal Focus: _____

Daily Affirmation: _____

_____

Reflective Journal Keywords: _____

_____

6th SATURDAY

Full Moon

Magickal Focus: _____

Daily Affirmation: _____

_____

Reflective Journal Keywords: _____

_____

7th SUNDAY

Magickal Focus: _____

Daily Affirmation: _____

_____

Reflective Journal Keywords: _____

_____

To do

September 2025

8th MONDAY	**9th TUESDAY**
Magickal Focus: _____ Daily Affirmation: _____ _____ Reflective Journal Keywords: _____ _____	Magickal Focus: _____ Daily Affirmation: _____ _____ Reflective Journal Keywords: _____ _____
10th WEDNESDAY	**11th THURSDAY**
Magickal Focus: _____ Daily Affirmation: _____ _____ Reflective Journal Keywords: _____ _____	Magickal Focus: _____ Daily Affirmation: _____ _____ Reflective Journal Keywords: _____ _____

12th FRIDAY

Magickal Focus: _____

Daily Affirmation: _____
_____

Reflective Journal Keywords: _____
_____

13th SATURDAY

Last Quarter Moon

Magickal Focus: _____

Daily Affirmation: _____
_____

Reflective Journal Keywords: _____
_____

14th SUNDAY

Magickal Focus: _____

Daily Affirmation: _____
_____

Reflective Journal Keywords: _____
_____

To do

September 2025

15th MONDAY

Magickal Focus: _____

Daily Affirmation: _____

Reflective Journal Keywords: _____

16th TUESDAY

Magickal Focus: _____

Daily Affirmation: _____

Reflective Journal Keywords: _____

17th WEDNESDAY

Magickal Focus: _____

Daily Affirmation: _____

Reflective Journal Keywords: _____

18th THURSDAY

Magickal Focus: _____

Daily Affirmation: _____

Reflective Journal Keywords: _____

19th FRIDAY

Magickal Focus: _____

Daily Affirmation: _____
_____

Reflective Journal Keywords: _____
_____

20th SATURDAY

Dark Moon

Magickal Focus: _____

Daily Affirmation: _____
_____

Reflective Journal Keywords: _____
_____

21st SUNDAY

Magickal Focus: _____

Daily Affirmation: _____
_____

Reflective Journal Keywords: _____
_____

To do

September 2025

22nd MONDAY	23rd TUESDAY
Autumn Equinox *Mabon* Magickal Focus:_____ Daily Affirmation:_____ _____ Reflective Journal Keywords:_____ _____	 Magickal Focus:_____ Daily Affirmation:_____ _____ Reflective Journal Keywords:_____ _____
24th WEDNESDAY	**25th THURSDAY**
        Magickal Focus:_____ Daily Affirmation:_____ _____ Reflective Journal Keywords:_____ _____	 Magickal Focus:_____ Daily Affirmation:_____ _____ Reflective Journal Keywords:_____ _____

witchcraftspellsmagick.com

26th FRIDAY	**27th SATURDAY**
Magickal Focus: _____	Magickal Focus: _____
Daily Affirmation: _____	Daily Affirmation: _____
Reflective Journal Keywords: _____	Reflective Journal Keywords: _____
28th SUNDAY *First Quarter Moon* Magickal Focus: _____ Daily Affirmation: _____ Reflective Journal Keywords: _____	**To do**

September 2025

29th **MONDAY**	30th **TUESDAY**
Magickal Focus: _____ Daily Affirmation: _____ Reflective Journal Keywords: _____	Magickal Focus: _____ Daily Affirmation: _____ Reflective Journal Keywords: _____
NOTES	**To do**

witchcraftspellsmagick.com

October 2025

Monday	Tuesday	Wednesday	Thursday	Friday
29	30	1	2	3
6 *Full Moon in Aries*	7	8	9	10
13 *Last Quarter Moon*	14	15	16	17
20	21	22	23	24
27	28 *First Quarter Moon*	29	30	31 *Samhain*
3	4	5	6	7

witchcraftspellsmagick.com

Saturday	Sunday
4	5
11	12
18	19 *Dark Moon*
25	26
1 *Samhain*	2
8	9

This Month

Lunar Cycle Intention:
_____
_____

Most Important Events:
1. _____
2. _____
3. _____
4. _____
5. _____

To Do List:
○ _____
○ _____
○ _____
○ _____
○ _____
○ _____
○ _____

Notes & Thoughts:

October 2025

SAMHAIN - Greater Witches' Sabbat

Samhain is celebrated on the evening of the 31st of October in the Northern Hemisphere and the 30th of April in the Southern Hemisphere. This festival marks the end of the harvest season and the impending onset of winter, a time to honor the spirits of the deceased.

Samhain signifies a time of transition, where the veil between the worlds of the living and the dead is at its thinnest. This period is ideal for reflecting on the past year, honoring those who have passed, and seeking guidance for the future. The festival is deeply connected to themes of death and rebirth, symbolizing the cyclical nature of life. As nature undergoes a profound transformation, Samhain heralds a time of introspection and renewal, where the seeds of new life lie dormant beneath the earth's surface, awaiting the return of the sun. Celebrate Samhain with your heart aglow with candlelight and spirits brimming with hope, embracing the perpetual cycle of life's rhythms and the promise of rejuvenation that Samhain brings.

This Month's
RITUAL INSPIRATION
TAROT - Tarot or Oracle Deck
Either work with your full deck or choose a particular card from your deck as an invocation of energy you would like to work with throughout the month.

SÉANCES - Spirit Mediumship
Samhain is a good time to communicate with spirits. Conducting séances during this period can enhance your connection with the spiritual realm.

SCRYING - Crystal ball, Mirror, Water and Flame
Scrying is known by various names such as seeing or peering. It is the practice of looking into a suitable medium to detect significant messages through visions. This ancient art can be performed with a crystal ball, mirror, water, or flame, allowing you to gain insights and guidance.

Tarot Reading

Monthly Tarot readings offer you valuable guidance and insight for the month ahead. To start, shuffle your cards for at least 30-40 seconds while focusing on a specific question or area of your life that you would like guidance on.

When you're ready, lay down the top three cards to represent the past, present, and future. For further details on tarot, visit witchcraftspellsmagick.com

Past	**Current**	**Future**
Where you have been.	*Where you are now.*	*Where you are going next.*

Deck: _____ Date: _____

Card 1 - Past: _____

_____

_____

Card 2 - Current: _____

_____

_____

Card 3 - Future: _____

_____

_____

October Magickal Correspondences

During October, the season deepens further into autumn, bringing profound transformation and introspection.

Samhain, celebrated at the end of the month, marks the thinning of the veil between worlds, a time to honor ancestors and connect with the spirit realm. This is a period for reflection, remembrance, and embracing the mysteries of life and death.

Animals - Bat, Cat, Crow, Fox, Owl, Wolf
Aromatics - Copal, Frankincense, Sage, Sandalwood, Sweet-grass, Wormwood
Colours - Black, Green, Orange, Purple, Red, White
Crystals - Amethyst, Bloodstone, Citrine, Jet, Obsidian, Onyx, Smoky quartz
Flowers - Chrysanthemum, Dandelion, Deadly Nightshade, Marigold, Rose, Thistle
Fruits + Vegetables - Apple, Carrot, Grape, Pomegranate, Pumpkin
Herbs - Basil, Mint, Mugwort, Rosemary, Sage, Thyme
Spices - Allspice, Cinnamon, Clove, Nutmeg
Trees - Acorn, Birch, Hazel, Oak, Willow

ALTAR CHECKLIST
Honoring the Dead, Ancestors, and Spitits
Altar Setup Basics - Start with the Elements:
Earth: Pentacle | Water: Chalice
Air: Incense or Diffuser | Fire: Candle

Additional Ideas:
- Tarot | Pendulum | Divination Tools
- Keys | Coins | Personal items | Photographs
- Heirlooms | Jewelry | Written letter
- Pumpkin | Fall/Autumn leaves
- Black candles
- Altar besom | Cauldron
- Obsidian sphere | Scrying mirror
- Crystal ball | Spirit/Ouija board
- Offerings

Notes & Thoughts:

witchcraftspellsmagick.com

Sketch Your Altar Setup

Altar Planning

Creating a monthly altar helps you align with the cycles of nature and set focused intentions for your magickal practices.

Use this template to plan and organize your altar setup, ensuring that each element supports your intention and enhances your connection to the energies of the month. Thoughtful planning and intentional arrangement of your altar will amplify your magick and help manifest your desired outcomes.

Intention: _____

Desired Outcome: _____

Notable Monthly Energies: _____

_____

Altar Aesthetics: _____

_____

_____

Altar Elements: _____

_____

Intentions

Utilize an intention to form the foundation of your manifestation, which means creating the desired outcome in accordance with your will. Intentions are the purpose or reason for why you are creating a spell or engaging in any magickal practice.

This may be for love, good fortune, or to banish something from your life. When starting spell work, focus on intentions connected to yourself only, not others.

Even good magick can take on a life of its own and be unexpected, often tripling in power and energy and coming back to you —good, bad, or in a twisted form. When the time is right, choose as many intentions and cast as many protection charms, wellness, success, good fortune, and hope for love or companionship as you can manifest each month.

Intentions are woven into spells—spells hold the energy and the intention, working by following the path of least resistance. Start slow and small rather than aiming for unstoppable tidal waves.

Intention Setting

This month, choose 1-4 intentions to focus on, whether for the entire month, lunar cycle, or one per week, depending on how much you practice.

Setting clear and focused intentions is crucial in your magickal practice. Narrowing your focus helps channel your energy more effectively. Whether for self-improvement, attracting positivity, or banishing negativity, these intentions guide your magickal work and keep you aligned with your goals.

Review and select your intentions this month. Consistency and clarity are key, allowing your intentions to manifest through dedicated practice, repetition, effort, and willpower.

Adventure	Authenticity	Balance
Calm	Career	Change
Comfort	Communication	Community
Culture	Divine wisdom	Education
Energy	Family	Freedom
Friends	Fun	Growth
Happiness	Health	Honesty
Honoring	Integrity	Knowledge
Peace	Relationships	Resilience
Respect	Security	Self
Success	Travel	Trust
Wealth	Will	Wisdom

Spell Casting
TRANSFORM AN INTENTION INTO A SPELL

Crafting a spell involves careful planning and aligning various elements that resonate with your desired outcome.

Utilize spells to transform your intentions into reality. Use this template to plan and organize your spell work. Ensure each component supports and aligns with your intention, enhancing your magick with energy. By thoughtfully and mindfully selecting and arranging spell elements, you can amplify your magick and increase the effectiveness of your spell work. With focused intent and deliberate action, you will manifest your desires and achieve your goals.

Making Magick

When casting spells, consider which energies support your intention. Determine which correspondences, moon phases, planetary alignments, seasons, or times of day are best. Carefully selecting these elements enhances your spell's power and effectiveness.

Repetition Magick

Repetition Magick involves repeating your entire spell multiple times to strengthen the likelihood of achieving your desired outcome. This intensifies the energy and makes your spell more effective. **Never spell and tell before a spell has worked! It can muddle and redirect your focused energy, leading to negative results.**

Spell 1

Intention: _____

_____

Desired Outcome: _____

_____

_____

_____

Correspondences: _____

_____

_____

_____

_____

_____

_____

witchcraftspellsmagick.com

Spell 2

Intention: _____

_____

Desired Outcome: _____

_____

_____

_____

Correspondences: _____

_____

_____

_____

_____

_____

_____

Spell 3

Intention: _____

_____

Desired Outcome: _____

_____

_____

_____

Correspondences: _____

_____

_____

_____

_____

_____

_____

Spells are the manifestation of your will!
Spells are a powerful tool for you to work with to manifest your desires. By setting a clear intention and casting a spell during a ritual, you can transform energy and bend outcomes to your will. These incantations, also known as enchantments or bewitchery, take many forms—spoken, written, thought, chanted, or sung. Successful spell work requires an alchemical mix of components and a lot of practice and patience. With dedication and focus, you can utilize the power of spells to create your desired outcome.

Ritual Preparation

SACRED SPACE AND CIRCLE CASTING STEPS

Cast a circle before spell and ritual work, or anytime you want to invoke protection and create a sacred space. Here are some steps to guide you:

1. Preparation
Collect objects and prepare your space for ritual or spell work.

2. Purification
Cleanse the space and yourself.

3. Casting
Create a physical or psychic circle for protection and manifestation.

4. Invocation
Introduce the energies you intend to work with. Invocation: *"I/we graciously invoke you..."*

5. Intention
Use your tool to draw a pentagram and state your intention.

6. Ritual Practice
Meditation, trance work, psychic divination, dance, chanting, spell work...

7. Closing
Dance, sing, or share offerings.

8. Gratitude and Reflection
Give thanks to the divine, metaphysical, elemental, spirit, and mortal energies you have worked with.

Ritual 1

Intention: _____

Desired Outcome: _____

Notable Monthly Energies: _____

_____

Altar Aesthetics: _____

_____

Altar Elements: _____

_____

_____

Ritual 2

Intention: _____

Desired Outcome: _____

Notable Monthly Energies: _____
_____

Altar Aesthetics: _____
_____

Altar Elements: _____
_____
_____

1. Preparation, 2. Purification, 3. Casting, 4. Invocation,
5. Intention, 6. Ritual Practice, 7. Closing, 8. Gratitude and Reflection

Ritual 3

Intention: _____

Desired Outcome: _____

Notable Monthly Energies: _____
_____

Altar Aesthetics: _____
_____

Altar Elements: _____
_____
_____

October 2025

To do	NOTES

1st WEDNESDAY	2nd THURSDAY
Magickal Focus: _____	Magickal Focus: _____
Daily Affirmation: _____	Daily Affirmation: _____
Reflective Journal Keywords: _____	Reflective Journal Keywords: _____

witchcraftspellsmagick.com

3rd FRIDAY

Magickal Focus: _____

Daily Affirmation: _____

_____

Reflective Journal Keywords: _____

_____

4th SATURDAY

Magickal Focus: _____

Daily Affirmation: _____

_____

Reflective Journal Keywords: _____

_____

5th SUNDAY

Magickal Focus: _____

Daily Affirmation: _____

_____

Reflective Journal Keywords: _____

_____

To do

October 2025

6th MONDAY	7th TUESDAY
Full Moon	
Magickal Focus: _____	Magickal Focus: _____
Daily Affirmation: _____	Daily Affirmation: _____
Reflective Journal Keywords: _____	Reflective Journal Keywords: _____
8th WEDNESDAY	**9th THURSDAY**
Magickal Focus: _____	Magickal Focus: _____
Daily Affirmation: _____	Daily Affirmation: _____
Reflective Journal Keywords: _____	Reflective Journal Keywords: _____

witchcraftspellsmagick.com

10th FRIDAY

Magickal Focus: _____

Daily Affirmation: _____
_____

Reflective Journal Keywords: _____
_____

11th SATURDAY

Magickal Focus: _____

Daily Affirmation: _____
_____

Reflective Journal Keywords: _____
_____

12th SUNDAY

Magickal Focus: _____

Daily Affirmation: _____
_____

Reflective Journal Keywords: _____
_____

To do

October 2025

13th MONDAY	14th TUESDAY
Last Quarter Moon Magickal Focus: _____ Daily Affirmation: _____ _____ Reflective Journal Keywords: _____ _____	 Magickal Focus: _____ Daily Affirmation: _____ _____ Reflective Journal Keywords: _____ _____
15th WEDNESDAY	**16th THURSDAY**
     Magickal Focus: _____ Daily Affirmation: _____ _____ Reflective Journal Keywords: _____ _____	 Magickal Focus: _____ Daily Affirmation: _____ _____ Reflective Journal Keywords: _____ _____

witchcraftspellsmagick.com

17th FRIDAY

Magickal Focus: _____

Daily Affirmation: _____

_____

Reflective Journal Keywords: _____

_____

18th SATURDAY

Magickal Focus: _____

Daily Affirmation: _____

_____

Reflective Journal Keywords: _____

_____

19th SUNDAY

Dark Moon

Magickal Focus: _____

Daily Affirmation: _____

_____

Reflective Journal Keywords: _____

_____

To do

October 2025

20th MONDAY	**21st TUESDAY**
Magickal Focus: _____ Daily Affirmation: _____ _____ Reflective Journal Keywords: _____ _____	Magickal Focus: _____ Daily Affirmation: _____ _____ Reflective Journal Keywords: _____ _____
22nd WEDNESDAY	**23rd THURSDAY**
Magickal Focus: _____ Daily Affirmation: _____ _____ Reflective Journal Keywords: _____ _____	Magickal Focus: _____ Daily Affirmation: _____ _____ Reflective Journal Keywords: _____ _____

witchcraftspellsmagick.com

24th FRIDAY

Magickal Focus: _____

Daily Affirmation: _____

_____

Reflective Journal Keywords: _____

_____

25th SATURDAY

Magickal Focus: _____

Daily Affirmation: _____

_____

Reflective Journal Keywords: _____

_____

26th SUNDAY

Magickal Focus: _____

Daily Affirmation: _____

_____

Reflective Journal Keywords: _____

_____

To do

October 2025

27th MONDAY	28th TUESDAY
	First Quarter Moon
Magickal Focus: _____	Magickal Focus: _____
Daily Affirmation: _____	Daily Affirmation: _____
Reflective Journal Keywords: _____	Reflective Journal Keywords: _____
29th WEDNESDAY	**30th THURSDAY**
Magickal Focus: _____	Magickal Focus: _____
Daily Affirmation: _____	Daily Affirmation: _____
Reflective Journal Keywords: _____	Reflective Journal Keywords: _____

witchcraftspellsmagick.com

31st FRIDAY

Samhain

Magickal Focus: _____

Daily Affirmation: _____

_____

Reflective Journal Keywords: _____

_____

NOTES

NOTES

To do

November 2025

Monday	Tuesday	Wednesday	Thursday	Friday
27	28	29	30	31 *Samhain*
3	4	5 *Full Moon in Taurus*	6	7
10	11 *Last Quarter Moon*	12	13	14
17	18 *First Quarter Moon*	19	20	21
24	25	26 *Dark Moon*	27	28
1	2	3	4	5

witchcraftspellsmagick.com

2025 Book of Shadows 297

Saturday	Sunday
1	2
8	9
15	16
22	23
29	30
6	7

This Month

Lunar Cycle Intention:

_____

_____

Most Important Events:

1. _____
2. _____
3. _____
4. _____
5. _____

To Do List:

○ _____
○ _____
○ _____
○ _____
○ _____
○ _____
○ _____

Notes & Thoughts:

November 2025

MOON ESBAT - Witches' Sabbat
The November Moon Esbat is observed on the 5th in the Northern Hemisphere and the 6th in the Southern Hemisphere. It is a sacred celebration focused on connecting with the Triple Goddess.

A Moon Esbat can be any ritual or magickal work performed during any moon phase, not just the full moon. These rituals offer an opportunity to attune to lunar energies and honor the phases of the moon. The Maiden represents the new moon, the Mother the full moon, and the Crone the waning moon. Esbats are ideal for deepening practice and connection between Sabbats.

During a full moon, emotions may be heightened, so it's crucial to make decisions based on rational thinking rather than impulsive feelings. The full moon acts as nature's catalyst, awakening from routine and offering new perspectives.

The moon, embodying femininity, provides a chance for sharing, teaching, healing, and learning. Esbats carry a distinct energy compared to Sabbats, contributing to a balanced and harmonious practice.

This Month's
RITUAL INSPIRATION
MOONLIGHT MEDITATION - Inner Peace and Clarity

Find a serene outdoor spot and sit under the moonlight. Close your eyes and take deep breaths, letting the moon's energy wash over you. Focus on clearing your mind and seeking inner peace. Visualize the moonlight illuminating your path forward.

LUNAR JOURNALING - Reflect and Manifest

Use the light of the moon to guide a journaling session. Write about your experiences, feelings, and goals. Reflect on the past month and set intentions for the coming weeks. The moon's energy can help bring clarity and inspire new ideas.

NIGHT GARDEN RITUAL - Connect with Nature

Spend time in your garden or a nearby natural space during the moon's peak. Plant seeds or tend to your plants, connecting with the earth and the moon's cycles.

witchcraftspellsmagick.com

Tarot Reading

Monthly Tarot readings offer you valuable guidance and insight for the month ahead. To start, shuffle your cards for at least 30-40 seconds while focusing on a specific question or area of your life that you would like guidance on.

When you're ready, lay down the top three cards to represent the past, present, and future. For further details on tarot, visit witchcraftspellsmagick.com

Past *Where you have been.*	**Current** *Where you are now.*	**Future** *Where you are going next.*

Deck: _____ **Date:** _____

Card 1 - Past: _____

_____

_____

Card 2 - Current: _____

_____

_____

Card 3 - Future: _____

_____

_____

November Magickal Correspondences

November welcomes in a time of introspection and preparational energies.

The days grow shorter and cooler, encouraging the reflection of life and the harvest of the year's efforts. This month is ideal for focusing on the Moon Esbat, celebrating the cycles of the moon and the deep connection between lunar energies and your magickal practices.

Animals - Bat, Deer, Fox, Owl, Rabbit, Wolf
Aromatics - Cedar, Cinnamon, Clove, Eucalyptus, Myrrh, Sage
Colours - Brown, Gold, Orange, Red, Yellow
Crystals - Amber, Bloodstone, Garnet, Obsidian, Smoky Quartz
Flowers - Aster, Chrysanthemum, Goldenrod, Marigold, Mums, Sunflower
Fruits + Vegetables - Apple, Beetroot, Carrot, Cranberry, Pumpkin, Sweet Potato
Herbs - Rosemary, Sage, Thyme, Mugwort, Mint, Basil, Oregano, Parsley, Tarragon
Spices - Allspice, Cardamom, Cinnamon, Clove, Ginger, Nutmeg, Star Anise
Trees - Birch, Cedar, Hickory, Maple, Oak, Pine

ALTAR CHECKLIST

Moon Esbat

Altar Setup Basics - Start with the Elements:

Earth: Pentacle | Water: Chalice

Air: Incense or Diffuser | Fire: Candle

Additional Ideas:
- Full moon symbol | Moon Goddess statue
- Seasonal flowers | Moon water
- Herbs (Rosemary, Sage)
- Ritual bowl | Symbols of harvest
- Silver jewelry | Feathers
- Offerings (Apple, Pomegranate)
- Journal or Book of Shadows
- Mirror
- Brown or orange cloth (altar covering)

Notes & Thoughts:

Sketch Your Altar Setup

Altar Planning

Creating a monthly altar helps you align with the cycles of nature and set focused intentions for your magickal practices.

Use this template to plan and organize your altar setup, ensuring that each element supports your intention and enhances your connection to the energies of the month. Thoughtful planning and intentional arrangement of your altar will amplify your magick and help manifest your desired outcomes.

Intention: _____

Desired Outcome: _____

Notable Monthly Energies: _____

_____

Altar Aesthetics: _____

_____

_____

Altar Elements: _____

_____

Intentions

Utilize an intention to form the foundation of your manifestation, which means creating the desired outcome in accordance with your will. Intentions are the purpose or reason for why you are creating a spell or engaging in any magickal practice.

This may be for love, good fortune, or to banish something from your life. When starting spell work, focus on intentions connected to yourself only, not others.

Even good magick can take on a life of its own and be unexpected, often tripling in power and energy and coming back to you —good, bad, or in a twisted form. When the time is right, choose as many intentions and cast as many protection charms, wellness, success, good fortune, and hope for love or companionship as you can manifest each month.

Intentions are woven into spells—spells hold the energy and the intention, working by following the path of least resistance. Start slow and small rather than aiming for unstoppable tidal waves.

Intention Setting

This month, choose 1-4 intentions to focus on, whether for the entire month, lunar cycle, or one per week, depending on how much you practice.

Setting clear and focused intentions is crucial in your magickal practice. Narrowing your focus helps channel your energy more effectively. Whether for self-improvement, attracting positivity, or banishing negativity, these intentions guide your magickal work and keep you aligned with your goals.

Review and select your intentions this month. Consistency and clarity are key, allowing your intentions to manifest through dedicated practice, repetition, effort, and willpower.

Adventure	Authenticity	Balance
Calm	Career	Change
Comfort	Communication	Community
Culture	Divine wisdom	Education
Energy	Family	Freedom
Friends	Fun	Growth
Happiness	Health	Honesty
Honoring	Integrity	Knowledge
Peace	Relationships	Resilience
Respect	Security	Self
Success	Travel	Trust
Wealth	Will	Wisdom

Spell Casting

TRANSFORM AN INTENTION INTO A SPELL

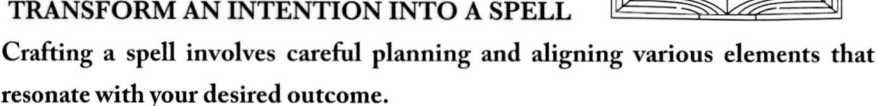

Crafting a spell involves careful planning and aligning various elements that resonate with your desired outcome.

Utilize spells to transform your intentions into reality. Use this template to plan and organize your spell work. Ensure each component supports and aligns with your intention, enhancing your magick with energy. By thoughtfully and mindfully selecting and arranging spell elements, you can amplify your magick and increase the effectiveness of your spell work. With focused intent and deliberate action, you will manifest your desires and achieve your goals.

Making Magick

When casting spells, consider which energies support your intention. Determine which correspondences, moon phases, planetary alignments, seasons, or times of day are best. Carefully selecting these elements enhances your spell's power and effectiveness.

Repetition Magick

Repetition Magick involves repeating your entire spell multiple times to strengthen the likelihood of achieving your desired outcome. This intensifies the energy and makes your spell more effective. **Never spell and tell before a spell has worked! It can muddle and redirect your focused energy, leading to negative results.**

Spell 1

Intention: _____

_____

Desired Outcome: _____

_____

_____

_____

Correspondences: _____

_____

_____

_____

_____

_____

_____

_____

witchcraftspellsmagick.com

Spell 2

Intention: _____

_____

Desired Outcome: _____

_____

_____

_____

Correspondences: _____

_____

_____

_____

_____

_____

_____

Spell 3

Intention: _____

_____

Desired Outcome: _____

_____

_____

_____

Correspondences: _____

_____

_____

_____

_____

_____

_____

Spells are the manifestation of your will!

Spells are a powerful tool for you to work with to manifest your desires. By setting a clear intention and casting a spell during a ritual, you can transform energy and bend outcomes to your will. These incantations, also known as enchantments or bewitchery, take many forms—spoken, written, thought, chanted, or sung. Successful spell work requires an alchemical mix of components and a lot of practice and patience. With dedication and focus, you can utilize the power of spells to create your desired outcome.

Ritual Preparation

SACRED SPACE AND CIRCLE CASTING STEPS

Cast a circle before spell and ritual work, or anytime you want to invoke protection and create a sacred space. Here are some steps to guide you:

1. Preparation
Collect objects and prepare your space for ritual or spell work.

2. Purification
Cleanse the space and yourself.

3. Casting
Create a physical or psychic circle for protection and manifestation.

4. Invocation
Introduce the energies you intend to work with. Invocation: *"I/we graciously invoke you..."*

5. Intention
Use your tool to draw a pentagram and state your intention.

6. Ritual Practice
Meditation, trance work, psychic divination, dance, chanting, spell work...

7. Closing
Dance, sing, or share offerings.

8. Gratitude and Reflection
Give thanks to the divine, metaphysical, elemental, spirit, and mortal energies you have worked with.

Ritual 1

Intention: _____

Desired Outcome: _____

Notable Monthly Energies: _____

_____

Altar Aesthetics: _____

_____

Altar Elements: _____

_____

_____

witchcraftspellsmagick.com

Ritual 2

Intention: _____

Desired Outcome: _____

Notable Monthly Energies: _____

_____

Altar Aesthetics: _____

_____

Altar Elements: _____

_____

_____

---

1. Preparation, 2. Purification, 3. Casting, 4. Invocation,
5. Intention, 6. Ritual Practice, 7. Closing, 8. Gratitude and Reflection

---

Ritual 3

Intention: _____

Desired Outcome: _____

Notable Monthly Energies: _____

_____

Altar Aesthetics: _____

_____

Altar Elements: _____

_____

_____

November 2025

To do	1st SATURDAY
	Samhain Magickal Focus: _____ Daily Affirmation: _____ _____ Reflective Journal Keywords: _____ _____
2nd SUNDAY Magickal Focus: _____ Daily Affirmation: _____ _____ Reflective Journal Keywords: _____ _____	**To do**

November 2025

3rd MONDAY	**4th TUESDAY**
Magickal Focus: _____ Daily Affirmation: _____ Reflective Journal Keywords: _____	Magickal Focus: _____ Daily Affirmation: _____ Reflective Journal Keywords: _____
5th WEDNESDAY *Full Moon*	**6th THURSDAY**
Magickal Focus: _____ Daily Affirmation: _____ Reflective Journal Keywords: _____	Magickal Focus: _____ Daily Affirmation: _____ Reflective Journal Keywords: _____

7th FRIDAY

Magickal Focus: _____

Daily Affirmation: _____
_____

Reflective Journal Keywords: _____
_____

8th SATURDAY

Magickal Focus: _____

Daily Affirmation: _____
_____

Reflective Journal Keywords: _____
_____

9th SUNDAY

Magickal Focus: _____

Daily Affirmation: _____
_____

Reflective Journal Keywords: _____
_____

To do

November 2025

10th MONDAY

Magickal Focus: _____

Daily Affirmation: _____

_____

Reflective Journal Keywords: _____

_____

11th TUESDAY

Last Quarter Moon

Magickal Focus: _____

Daily Affirmation: _____

_____

Reflective Journal Keywords: _____

_____

12th WEDNESDAY

Magickal Focus: _____

Daily Affirmation: _____

_____

Reflective Journal Keywords: _____

_____

13th THURSDAY

Magickal Focus: _____

Daily Affirmation: _____

_____

Reflective Journal Keywords: _____

_____

witchcraftspellsmagick.com

14th FRIDAY

Magickal Focus: _____

Daily Affirmation: _____

_____

Reflective Journal Keywords: _____

_____

15th SATURDAY

Magickal Focus: _____

Daily Affirmation: _____

_____

Reflective Journal Keywords: _____

_____

16th SUNDAY

Magickal Focus: _____

Daily Affirmation: _____

_____

Reflective Journal Keywords: _____

_____

To do

November 2025

17th MONDAY	18th TUESDAY
	Dark Moon
Magickal Focus: _____	Magickal Focus: _____
Daily Affirmation: _____	Daily Affirmation: _____
Reflective Journal Keywords: _____	Reflective Journal Keywords: _____
19th WEDNESDAY	**20th THURSDAY**
Magickal Focus: _____	Magickal Focus: _____
Daily Affirmation: _____	Daily Affirmation: _____
Reflective Journal Keywords: _____	Reflective Journal Keywords: _____

witchcraftspellsmagick.com

21st FRIDAY	**22nd SATURDAY**
Magickal Focus: _____ Daily Affirmation: _____ _____ Reflective Journal Keywords: _____ _____	Magickal Focus: _____ Daily Affirmation: _____ _____ Reflective Journal Keywords: _____ _____
23rd SUNDAY	**To do**
Magickal Focus: _____ Daily Affirmation: _____ _____ Reflective Journal Keywords: _____ _____	

November 2025

24th MONDAY	**25th TUESDAY**
Magickal Focus: _____	Magickal Focus: _____
Daily Affirmation: _____	Daily Affirmation: _____
_____	_____
Reflective Journal Keywords: _____	Reflective Journal Keywords: _____
_____	_____
26th WEDNESDAY	**27th THURSDAY**
First Quarter Moon	
Magickal Focus: _____	Magickal Focus: _____
Daily Affirmation: _____	Daily Affirmation: _____
_____	_____
Reflective Journal Keywords: _____	Reflective Journal Keywords: _____
_____	_____

witchcraftspellsmagick.com

28th FRIDAY	**29th SATURDAY**
Magickal Focus:_____	Magickal Focus:_____
Daily Affirmation: _____	Daily Affirmation: _____
Reflective Journal Keywords: _____	Reflective Journal Keywords: _____
30th SUNDAY	**To do**
Magickal Focus:_____	
Daily Affirmation: _____	
Reflective Journal Keywords: _____	

December 2025

Monday	Tuesday	Wednesday	Thursday	Friday
24	25	26	27	28
1	2	3	4 *Full Moon in Gemini*	5
8	9	10	11 *Last Quarter Moon*	12
15	16	17	18 *Dark Moon*	19
22	23	24	25	26 *First Quarter Moon*
29	30	31	1	2

witchcraftspellsmagick.com

Saturday	Sunday
29	30
6	7
13	14
20	21 *Winter solstice* *Yule*
27	28
3	4

This Month

Lunar Cycle Intention:

_____
_____

Most Important Events:

1. _____
2. _____
3. _____
4. _____
5. _____

To Do List:

○ _____
○ _____
○ _____
○ _____
○ _____
○ _____
○ _____

Notes & Thoughts:

December 2025

WINTER SOLSTICE | YULE - Lesser Witches' Sabbat

Yule in the Northern Hemisphere is observed on the Winter Solstice, the 21st of December with the 12 days of Yuletide celebrated until the 1st of January. In the Southern Hemisphere, Yule falls on the 21st of June.

This festival celebrates the sun's rebirth after the long, cold winter months, symbolizing renewal and the promise of new life.

Yule is a time to honor the natural world, which has entered a period of dormancy and will soon be reborn, emerging renewed and full of life. Traditions include decorating with greenery, lighting Yule logs nightly, sharing meals, and giving gifts, symbolizing the rebirth of nature and the warmth of community spirit.

The 'Twelve Nights of Yuletide,' from the 21st of December to the 1st of January, is a festival of Pagan origin, with the tradition of taking down decorations by the 12th day to avoid bad luck. As you gather to celebrate Yuletide, embrace the warmth of community, the joy of giving, and the light of the reborn sun, reflecting on the cycles of nature and the promise of renewal that Yuletide brings.

This Month's
RITUAL INSPIRATION

WREATH MAKING - Magickal Herb Wreath

Using herbs and flowers, make a wreath to honor the passing of the shortest day during Yule. The round shape symbolizes victory and honor in Pagan tradition.

YULE LOG - Bless the Return of the Sun

Burn a Yule log for good luck and protection. Light it for 'The 12 Nights of Yuletide,' from December 21st to January 1st, reflecting with gratitude each night.

DECORATE A YULE TREE - Remembering Ancestors

Add decorations to a living tree, outside if possible. Consider homemade Pagan crafts made from recycled or reused materials. This act honors your ancestors and embraces the traditions of Yule.

witchcraftspellsmagick.com

Tarot Reading

Monthly Tarot readings offer you valuable guidance and insight for the month ahead. To start, shuffle your cards for at least 30-40 seconds while focusing on a specific question or area of your life that you would like guidance on.

When you're ready, lay down the top three cards to represent the past, present, and future. For further details on tarot, visit witchcraftspellsmagick.com

Past
Where you have been.

Current
Where you are now.

Future
Where you are going next.

Deck: _____ **Date:** _____

Card 1 - Past: _____

_____

_____

Card 2 - Current: _____

_____

_____

Card 3 - Future: _____

_____

_____

December Magickal Correspondences

During December in the Northern Hemisphere, the season transitions into winter, a time of introspection and transformation.

Yule, the Winter Solstice, marks the longest night and the rebirth of the sun, symbolizing hope and renewal. This is a period to celebrate the return of light and the promise of new beginnings, aligning with December's energies of rebirth and renewal.

Animals - Cat, Deer, Fox, Goat, Owl, Robin, Squirrel
Aromatics - Carnation, Frankincense, Lavender, Myrrh, Sandalwood, Sweet orange
Colours - Blue, Dark green, Gold, Purple, Red, Silver, White
Crystals - Amethyst, Bloodstone, Clear quartz, Diamond, Emerald, Garnet, Ruby,
Flowers - Chamomile, Edelweiss, Lavender, Rose
Fruits - Apple, Berry, Orange, Pear
Herbs - Basil, Peppermint, Rosemary, Sage, Thyme
Spices - Allspice, Cinnamon, Clove, Ginger, Nutmeg
Trees - Birch, Cedar, Cypress, Evergreen, Holly, Juniper, Maple, Oak, Pine, Spruce

---

ALTAR CHECKLIST
Hope, Renewal and Rebirth
Altar Setup Basics - Start with the Elements:
Earth: Pentacle | Water: Chalice
Air: Incense or Diffuser | Fire: Candle

Additional Ideas:
- Wreath | Yule log
- Mistletoe | Yule tree | Holly | Evergreen
- Bells | Candles
- Gingerbread | Clove | Cinnamon sticks
- Pine cones | Ivy | Oak leaves
- Red, Green and Gold decorations
- Symbol of rebirth (phoenix, sun)
- Star or sun symbols
- Offering bowl

Notes & Thoughts:

Sketch Your Altar Setup

Altar Planning

Creating a monthly altar helps you align with the cycles of nature and set focused intentions for your magickal practices.

Use this template to plan and organize your altar setup, ensuring that each element supports your intention and enhances your connection to the energies of the month. Thoughtful planning and intentional arrangement of your altar will amplify your magick and help manifest your desired outcomes.

Intention: _____

Desired Outcome: _____

Notable Monthly Energies: _____

_____

Altar Aesthetics: _____

_____

_____

Altar Elements: _____

_____

Intentions

Utilize an intention to form the foundation of your manifestation, which means creating the desired outcome in accordance with your will. Intentions are the purpose or reason for why you are creating a spell or engaging in any magickal practice.

This may be for love, good fortune, or to banish something from your life. When starting spell work, focus on intentions connected to yourself only, not others.

Even good magick can take on a life of its own and be unexpected, often tripling in power and energy and coming back to you —good, bad, or in a twisted form. When the time is right, choose as many intentions and cast as many protection charms, wellness, success, good fortune, and hope for love or companionship as you can manifest each month.

Intentions are woven into spells—spells hold the energy and the intention, working by following the path of least resistance. Start slow and small rather than aiming for unstoppable tidal waves.

Intention Setting

This month, choose 1-4 intentions to focus on, whether for the entire month, lunar cycle, or one per week, depending on how much you practice.

Setting clear and focused intentions is crucial in your magickal practice. Narrowing your focus helps channel your energy more effectively. Whether for self-improvement, attracting positivity, or banishing negativity, these intentions guide your magickal work and keep you aligned with your goals.

Review and select your intentions this month. Consistency and clarity are key, allowing your intentions to manifest through dedicated practice, repetition, effort, and willpower.

Adventure	Authenticity	Balance
Calm	Career	Change
Comfort	Communication	Community
Culture	Divine wisdom	Education
Energy	Family	Freedom
Friends	Fun	Growth
Happiness	Health	Honesty
Honoring	Integrity	Knowledge
Peace	Relationships	Resilience
Respect	Security	Self
Success	Travel	Trust
Wealth	Will	Wisdom

Spell Casting

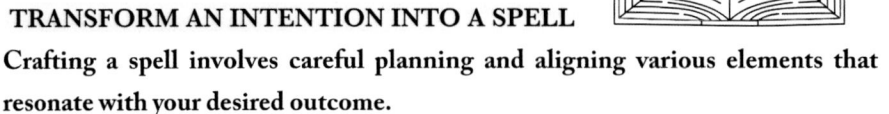

TRANSFORM AN INTENTION INTO A SPELL

Crafting a spell involves careful planning and aligning various elements that resonate with your desired outcome.

Utilize spells to transform your intentions into reality. Use this template to plan and organize your spell work. Ensure each component supports and aligns with your intention, enhancing your magick with energy. By thoughtfully and mindfully selecting and arranging spell elements, you can amplify your magick and increase the effectiveness of your spell work. With focused intent and deliberate action, you will manifest your desires and achieve your goals.

Making Magick

When casting spells, consider which energies support your intention. Determine which correspondences, moon phases, planetary alignments, seasons, or times of day are best. Carefully selecting these elements enhances your spell's power and effectiveness.

Repetition Magick

Repetition Magick involves repeating your entire spell multiple times to strengthen the likelihood of achieving your desired outcome. This intensifies the energy and makes your spell more effective. **Never spell and tell before a spell has worked! It can muddle and redirect your focused energy, leading to negative results.**

Spell 1

Intention: _____

_____

Desired Outcome: _____

_____

_____

Correspondences: _____

_____

_____

_____

_____

_____

_____

witchcraftspellsmagick.com

Spell 2

Intention: _____

_____

Desired Outcome: _____

_____

_____

_____

Correspondences: _____

_____

_____

_____

_____

_____

_____

Spell 3

Intention: _____

_____

Desired Outcome: _____

_____

_____

_____

Correspondences: _____

_____

_____

_____

_____

_____

_____

Spells are the manifestation of your will!
Spells are a powerful tool for you to work with to manifest your desires. By setting a clear intention and casting a spell during a ritual, you can transform energy and bend outcomes to your will. These incantations, also known as enchantments or bewitchery, take many forms—spoken, written, thought, chanted, or sung. Successful spell work requires an alchemical mix of components and a lot of practice and patience. With dedication and focus, you can utilize the power of spells to create your desired outcome.

Ritual Preparation

SACRED SPACE AND CIRCLE CASTING STEPS

Cast a circle before spell and ritual work, **or anytime you want to invoke protection and create a sacred space.** Here are some steps to guide you:

1. Preparation
Collect objects and prepare your space for ritual or spell work.

2. Purification
Cleanse the space and yourself.

3. Casting
Create a physical or psychic circle for protection and manifestation.

4. Invocation
Introduce the energies you intend to work with. Invocation: *"I/we graciously invoke you..."*

5. Intention
Use your tool to draw a pentagram and state your intention.

6. Ritual Practice
Meditation, trance work, psychic divination, dance, chanting, spell work...

7. Closing
Dance, sing, or share offerings.

8. Gratitude and Reflection
Give thanks to the divine, metaphysical, elemental, spirit, and mortal energies you have worked with.

Ritual 1

Intention: _____

Desired Outcome: _____

Notable Monthly Energies: _____

_____

Altar Aesthetics: _____

_____

Altar Elements: _____

_____

_____

witchcraftspellsmagick.com

Ritual 2

Intention: _____

Desired Outcome: _____

Notable Monthly Energies: _____

_____

Altar Aesthetics: _____

_____

Altar Elements: _____

_____

_____

1. Preparation, 2. Purification, 3. Casting, 4. Invocation,
5. Intention, 6. Ritual Practice, 7. Closing, 8. Gratitude and Reflection

Ritual 3

Intention: _____

Desired Outcome: _____

Notable Monthly Energies: _____

_____

Altar Aesthetics: _____

_____

Altar Elements: _____

_____

_____

December 2025

1st MONDAY

Magickal Focus: _____

Daily Affirmation: _____

_____

Reflective Journal Keywords: _____

_____

2nd TUESDAY

Magickal Focus: _____

Daily Affirmation: _____

_____

Reflective Journal Keywords: _____

_____

3rd WEDNESDAY

Magickal Focus: _____

Daily Affirmation: _____

_____

Reflective Journal Keywords: _____

_____

4th THURSDAY

Full Moon

Magickal Focus: _____

Daily Affirmation: _____

_____

Reflective Journal Keywords: _____

_____

witchcraftspellsmagick.com

5th FRIDAY

Magickal Focus: _____

Daily Affirmation: _____

_____

Reflective Journal Keywords: _____

_____

6th SATURDAY

Magickal Focus: _____

Daily Affirmation: _____

_____

Reflective Journal Keywords: _____

_____

7th SUNDAY

Magickal Focus: _____

Daily Affirmation: _____

_____

Reflective Journal Keywords: _____

_____

To do

December 2025

8th MONDAY

Magickal Focus: _____

Daily Affirmation: _____

_____

Reflective Journal Keywords: _____

_____

9th TUESDAY

Magickal Focus: _____

Daily Affirmation: _____

_____

Reflective Journal Keywords: _____

_____

10th WEDNESDAY

Magickal Focus: _____

Daily Affirmation: _____

_____

Reflective Journal Keywords: _____

_____

11th THURSDAY

Last Quarter Moon

Magickal Focus: _____

Daily Affirmation: _____

_____

Reflective Journal Keywords: _____

_____

12th FRIDAY

Magickal Focus: _____

Daily Affirmation: _____

_____

Reflective Journal Keywords: _____

_____

13th SATURDAY

Magickal Focus: _____

Daily Affirmation: _____

_____

Reflective Journal Keywords: _____

_____

14th SUNDAY

Magickal Focus: _____

Daily Affirmation: _____

_____

Reflective Journal Keywords: _____

_____

To do

December 2025

15th MONDAY

Magickal Focus: _____

Daily Affirmation: _____

_____

Reflective Journal Keywords: _____

_____

16th TUESDAY

Magickal Focus: _____

Daily Affirmation: _____

_____

Reflective Journal Keywords: _____

_____

17th WEDNESDAY

Magickal Focus: _____

Daily Affirmation: _____

_____

Reflective Journal Keywords: _____

_____

18th THURSDAY

Dark Moon

Magickal Focus: _____

Daily Affirmation: _____

_____

Reflective Journal Keywords: _____

_____

witchcraftspellsmagick.com

19th FRIDAY

Magickal Focus: _____

Daily Affirmation: _____

_____

Reflective Journal Keywords: _____

_____

20th SATURDAY

Magickal Focus: _____

Daily Affirmation: _____

_____

Reflective Journal Keywords: _____

_____

21st SUNDAY

Winter solstice
Yule

Magickal Focus: _____

Daily Affirmation: _____

_____

Reflective Journal Keywords: _____

_____

To do

December 2025

22nd MONDAY	23rd TUESDAY
Magickal Focus: _____ Daily Affirmation: _____ _____ Reflective Journal Keywords: _____ _____	Magickal Focus: _____ Daily Affirmation: _____ _____ Reflective Journal Keywords: _____ _____
24th WEDNESDAY	**25th THURSDAY**
Magickal Focus: _____ Daily Affirmation: _____ _____ Reflective Journal Keywords: _____ _____	Magickal Focus: _____ Daily Affirmation: _____ _____ Reflective Journal Keywords: _____ _____

witchcraftspellsmagick.com

26th FRIDAY	27th SATURDAY
First Quarter Moon	
Magickal Focus: _____	Magickal Focus: _____
Daily Affirmation: _____	Daily Affirmation: _____
Reflective Journal Keywords: _____	Reflective Journal Keywords: _____

28th SUNDAY	To do
Magickal Focus: _____	
Daily Affirmation: _____	
Reflective Journal Keywords: _____	

December 2025

29th MONDAY

Magickal Focus: _____

Daily Affirmation: _____
_____

Reflective Journal Keywords: _____
_____

30th TUESDAY

Magickal Focus: _____

Daily Affirmation: _____
_____

Reflective Journal Keywords: _____
_____

31st WEDNESDAY

Magickal Focus: _____

Daily Affirmation: _____
_____

Reflective Journal Keywords: _____
_____

To do

witchcraftspellsmagick.com

PART 5

Dreams

**"Your visions will become clear
only when you can look into your own heart.
Who looks outside, dreams; who looks inside, awakes."**
— *Dr. Carl Jung, Founder of Analytical Psychology*

Your subconscious mind knows things that the conscious mind is yet to realize, process, or understand. Tapping into your dreams and unveiling their deeply intuitive and insightful knowledge can help you in your waking life.

Understanding your dreams can be a challenge; our rational minds often determine meanings that aren't as they seem.

Dreams that uncover fears and negative experiences possess a deep purpose. Your unconscious often uses concepts that are deliberately meant to shake us up in our waking life.

Journaling your dreams will help you recall them, process them, and understand their deep messaging to support your waking life.

For dream meanings, refer to 'Dream Books' by Carl Jung or visit www.dreammoods.com.

Dream Journal

Dream Interpretation; either 'Dream Books' by Dr Carl Jung or visit www.dreammoods.com

Date: _____ **How do you feel about the dream?** _____
_____
_____

List any symbols or images: _____
_____
_____
_____

Describe the narrative: _____
_____
_____
_____
_____
_____
_____
_____

What is your intuitive understanding? _____
_____
_____

What is the interpreted meaning? _____
_____
_____

Dream Journal

Dream Interpretation; either 'Dream Books' by Dr Carl Jung or visit www.dreammoods.com

Date: _____ How do you feel about the dream? _____
_____
_____

List any symbols or images: _____
_____
_____
_____

Describe the narrative: _____
_____
_____
_____
_____
_____
_____
_____

What is your intuitive understanding? _____
_____
_____

What is the interpreted meaning? _____
_____
_____
_____

Dream Journal

Dream Interpretation; either 'Dream Books' by Dr Carl Jung or visit www.dreammoods.com

Date: _____ **How do you feel about the dream?** _____

_____

_____

List any symbols or images: _____

_____

_____

_____

Describe the narrative: _____

_____

_____

_____

_____

_____

_____

What is your intuitive understanding? _____

_____

_____

What is the interpreted meaning? _____

_____

_____

_____

witchcraftspellsmagick.com

Dream Journal

Dream Interpretation; either 'Dream Books' by Dr Carl Jung or visit www.dreammoods.com

Date: _____ **How do you feel about the dream?** _____

_____

_____

List any symbols or images: _____

_____

_____

_____

Describe the narrative: _____

_____

_____

_____

_____

_____

_____

What is your intuitive understanding? _____

_____

_____

What is the interpreted meaning? _____

_____

_____

Dream Journal

Dream Interpretation; either 'Dream Books' by Dr Carl Jung or visit www.dreammoods.com

Date: _____ **How do you feel about the dream?** _____

_____

_____

List any symbols or images: _____

_____

_____

_____

Describe the narrative: _____

_____

_____

_____

_____

_____

_____

What is your intuitive understanding? _____

_____

_____

What is the interpreted meaning? _____

_____

_____

_____

witchcraftspellsmagick.com

Dream Journal

Dream Interpretation; either 'Dream Books' by Dr Carl Jung or visit www.dreammoods.com

Date: _____ **How do you feel about the dream?** _____

_____

_____

List any symbols or images: _____

_____

_____

_____

Describe the narrative: _____

_____

_____

_____

_____

_____

_____

_____

What is your intuitive understanding? _____

_____

_____

What is the interpreted meaning? _____

_____

_____

_____

Dream Journal

Dream Interpretation; either 'Dream Books' by Dr Carl Jung or visit www.dreammoods.com

Date: _____ **How do you feel about the dream?** _____

_____

_____

List any symbols or images: _____

_____

_____

_____

Describe the narrative: _____

_____

_____

_____

_____

_____

_____

_____

What is your intuitive understanding? _____

_____

_____

What is the interpreted meaning? _____

_____

_____

_____

Dream Journal

Dream Interpretation; either 'Dream Books' by Dr Carl Jung or visit www.dreammoods.com

Date: _____ **How do you feel about the dream?** _____
_____
_____

List any symbols or images: _____
_____
_____
_____

Describe the narrative: _____
_____
_____
_____
_____
_____
_____
_____

What is your intuitive understanding? _____
_____
_____

What is the interpreted meaning? _____
_____
_____
_____

Dream Journal

Dream Interpretation; either 'Dream Books' by Dr Carl Jung or visit www.dreammoods.com

Date: _____ **How do you feel about the dream?** _____

_____

_____

List any symbols or images: _____

_____

_____

_____

Describe the narrative: _____

_____

_____

_____

_____

_____

_____

What is your intuitive understanding? _____

_____

_____

What is the interpreted meaning? _____

_____

_____

Dream Journal

Dream Interpretation; either 'Dream Books' by Dr Carl Jung or visit www.dreammoods.com

Date: _____ **How do you feel about the dream?** _____

_____

_____

List any symbols or images: _____

_____

_____

_____

Describe the narrative: _____

_____

_____

_____

_____

_____

_____

_____

What is your intuitive understanding? _____

_____

_____

_____

What is the interpreted meaning? _____

_____

_____

_____

Dream Journal

Dream Interpretation; either 'Dream Books' by Dr Carl Jung or visit www.dreammoods.com

Date: _____ **How do you feel about the dream?** _____
_____
_____

List any symbols or images: _____
_____
_____
_____

Describe the narrative: _____
_____
_____
_____
_____
_____
_____

What is your intuitive understanding? _____
_____
_____

What is the interpreted meaning? _____
_____
_____
_____

witchcraftspellsmagick.com

witchcraftspellsmagick.com

Witchcraft Spells Magick
witchcraftspellsmagick.com

WITCHCRAFT ACADEMY
Teaching Witches their Craft

Private Coven Group

Your invitation to Join!

www.witchcraftspellsmagick.com/pages/coven

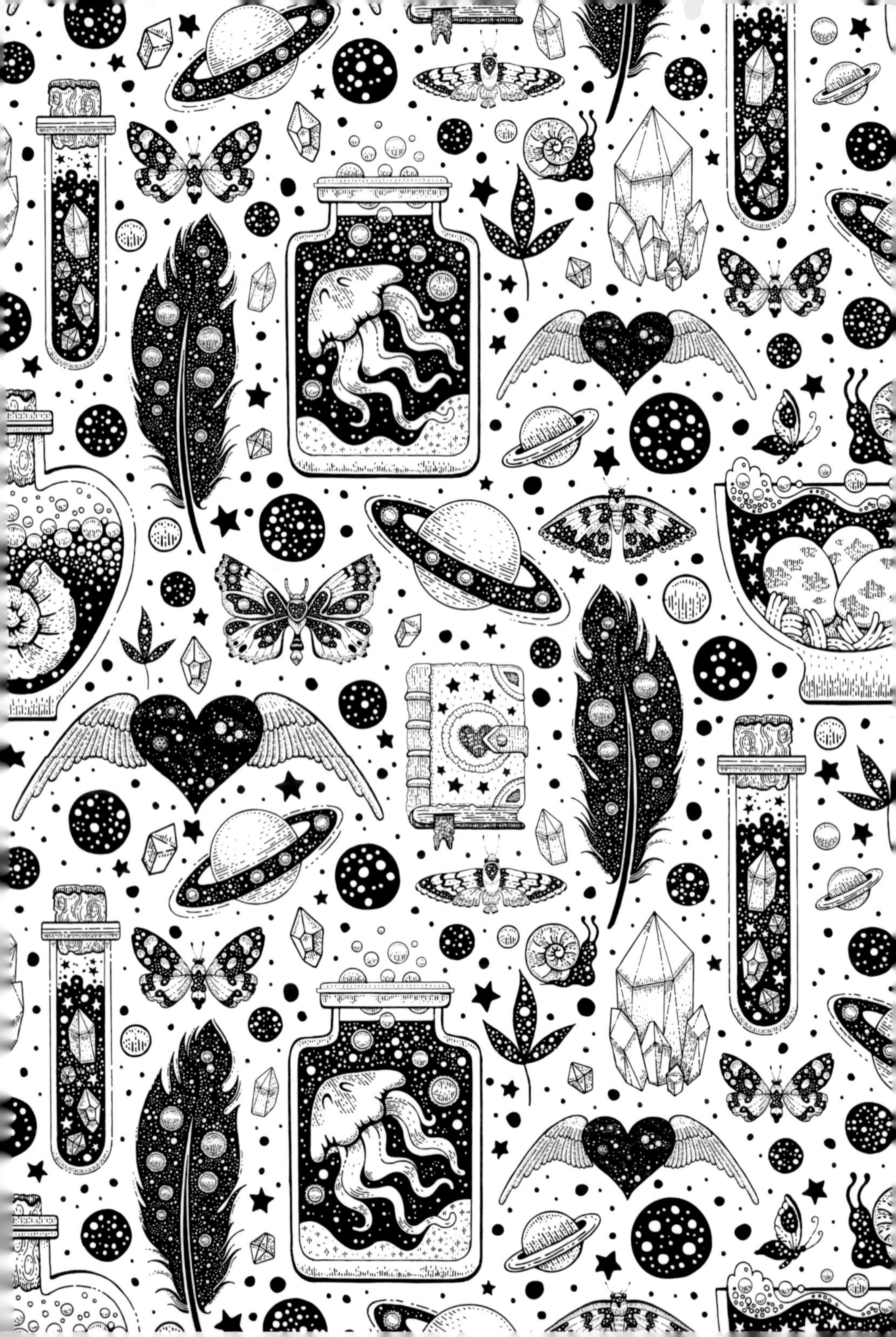

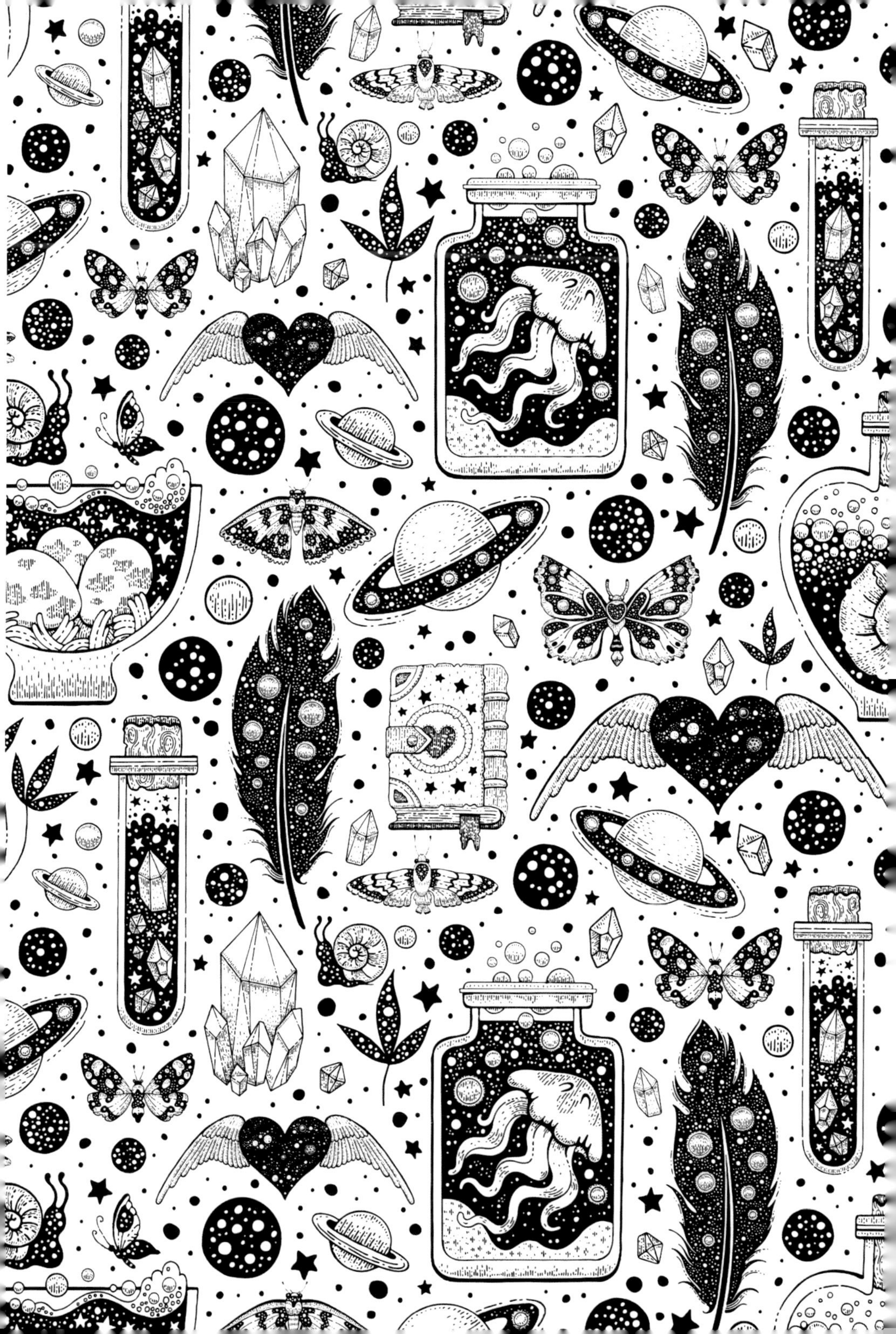

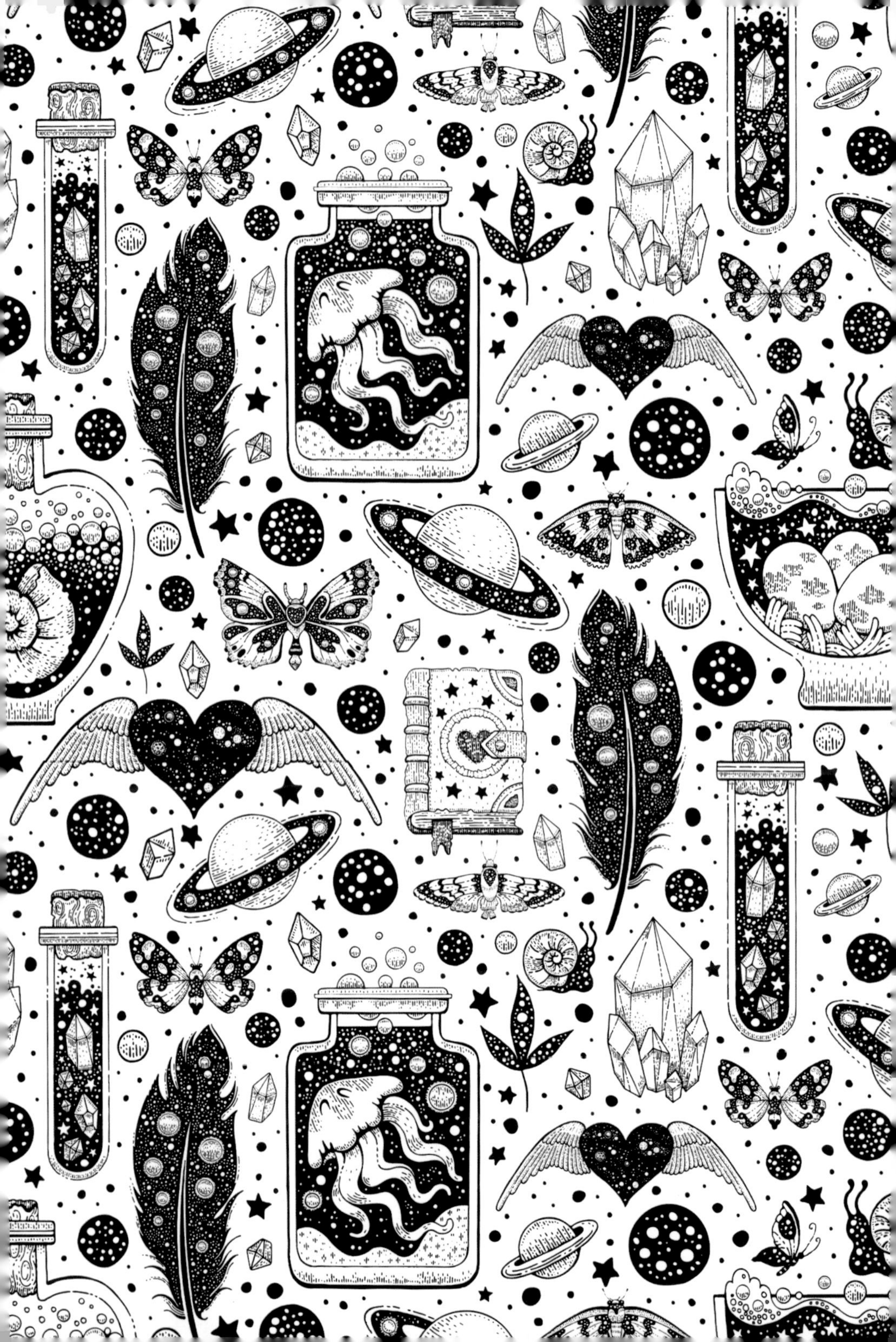

Milton Keynes UK
Ingram Content Group UK Ltd.
UKRC032033061224
452198UK00003B/1